OPERATION
FALL WEISS

GERMAN PARATROOPERS IN THE POLAND CAMPAIGN, 1939

OPERATION
FALL WEISS

GERMAN PARATROOPERS IN
THE POLAND CAMPAIGN, 1939

STEPHAN JANZYK
Translated by Susan Haynes-Huber

Pen & Sword
MILITARY

Originally published by VS Books Torsten Verhülsdonk in 2015 as
Deckname Fall Weiss
Deutsche Fallschirmjäger im Polenfeldzug 1939

First published in Great Britain in 2017 by
Pen & Sword Military
An imprint of
Pen & Sword Books Ltd
47 Church Street
Barnsley
South Yorkshire
S70 2AS

ISBN 978 1 47389 461 7

Typeset by Aura Technology and Software Services, India
Printed and bound in India by Replika Press Pvt. Ltd.

Pen & Sword Books Ltd incorporates the Imprints of Pen & Sword Books Archaeology,
Atlas, Aviation, Battleground, Discovery, Family History, History, Maritime, Military,
Naval, Politics, Railways, Select, Transport, True Crime, Fiction, Frontline Books,
Leo Cooper, Praetorian Press, Seaforth Publishing, Wharncliffe and White Owl.

For a complete list of Pen & Sword titles please contact
PEN & SWORD BOOKS LIMITED
47 Church Street, Barnsley, South Yorkshire, S70 2AS, England
E-mail: enquiries@pen-and-sword.co.uk
Website: www.pen-and-sword.co.uk

Contents

Acknowledgements

First of all, I would like to take the opportunity to thank those people without whom this book would probably never have been written. I owe a particular debt of thanks to my fellow collector and supporter, Sven Jordan. Thank you for your help with our mutual hobby and for the many, many pleasurable hours spent 'talking shop'. I would also like to thank the following collectors and historians: Edgar Alcidi, Marc Branzke, Hugo F. van Dijk, Philipp Engels, John Hodgkin, Chris Mason, Eric Queen, Gustav Skvaril, Thomas Steinke, Sören Szameitat and Shaun Winkler.

Thank you, too, to the ever-courteous and ever-helpful staff of the Federal Archive in Freiburg. Our many telephone calls and your intensive research made this book possible. Furthermore, I would like to thank the publishing house VS-BOOKS for the realisation of this project and for our successful collaboration.

And last but not least, I thank my wife and family for their patience and understanding, because we all know a hobby and project like this eats up a lot of time.

Stephan Janzyk

Introduction

Historical background

In the 1920s, following the end of the First World War in 1918 and the associated changes in national boundaries, which were in part stipulated by the Treaty of Versailles, many high-ranking politicians and statesmen saw the hope of a peaceful future already dwindling.

British Prime Minster Lloyd George, for example, stated in 1919: 'Redrawing boundaries in the East, placing more than two million Germans under Polish control, must, in my judgement, lead sooner or later to a new war in the East of Europe.'

In the Weimar Republic, foreign minister Gustav Stresemann and well-known Social Democrat and Prime Minister Otto Braun also attempted to defuse this potential source of conflict, first, with the approval of the French and British governments, by entering into renegotiations with the Polish heads of state. When these negotiations repeatedly failed, as Poland was understandably wary of a Weimar Republic which was becoming increasingly strong, France and Great Britain began to recognise and confirm the new boundaries.

With the beginning of the Great Depression in 1929 and the problems it brought with it for relations between states, the National Socialists seized their opportunity. An extremely nationalistic and aggressive political programme enabled them to seize power in Germany by 1933.

The social-Darwinist and geo-political aims they proclaimed found favour with a large proportion of the population. As a result of the 'Dolchstoßlegende,' for example, the stab-in-the-back myth which claimed that the German Army had, in fact, remained undefeated in the field in the First World War, or as a result of high unemployment resulting from the Great Depression, many saw the Treaty of Versailles and Germany's position within Europe as an extreme injustice that could only be remedied by means of a tough and expansionist policy under a strong leader.

On 26 January 1934, despite its obvious foreign policy objectives, the National Socialist government of the German Reich signed a non-aggression pact with Poland for the following ten years, which was completely contrary to the renegotiation policy of the former Weimar Republic.

With the Hoßbach Memorandum of November 1937, however, it became absolutely clear that despite the pact, Hitler was set on resolving the question of 'Lebensraum' in the East.

Preparations for war

Intensive rearmament of the Wehrmacht from 1935 onwards, clear violations of the Treaty of Versailles, the re-militarisation of the Rhineland in 1936, the annexation of Austria and the separation of German-speaking Sudetenland in 1938, ended the so-called appeasement policy of France and Great Britain.

Until now, France and Great Britain had striven to limit or halt Germany's expansion by political means. Both European powers emphasised their position with regard to Poland by issuing 'guarantees' of Polish independence. As far as military policy was concerned, Hitler, who had originally tried to interest Poland, with which it shared a border, in forming an alliance against the Soviet Union, drew the short straw.

In order to protect itself against possible armed intervention by the guarantor powers, Nazi Germany signed a non-aggression pact with the Soviet Union on 24 August 1939. German foreign minister Joachim von Ribbentrop flew to Moscow to negotiate dangerous agreements with the Russian foreign minister, Vyacheslav Michailovich Molotov. In fact, the pact already included a secret protocol outlining how the two powers would split Poland between them following a war. And four months before, on 3 April 1939, the high command of the Wehrmacht had already received instructions to begin preparations for a 'likely war with Poland.'

The outbreak of war

The Second World War began on 1 September 1939, without a prior declaration of war, when the forces of the German Wehrmacht began their invasion of Poland. Attempts were made to justify the invasion in the eyes of the world with the help of several false-flag operations along the German-Polish border, staged by the SS and SD and creating the impression of Polish aggression against Germany.

In this way, National Socialist Germany portrayed its attack on Poland, which was in violation of international law, as a counter-offensive. In advance, the SS had staged so-called border violations in which, for example, SS agents posing as Polish troops attacked two Silesian customs posts and the Gleiwitz German radio station. The idea was to create the impression that Germany had been forced to intervene.

When the old German battleship SMS *Schleswig-Holstein* began its bombardment of a Polish ammunition depot on the peninsula of Westerplatte in the port of Danzig at 4.45 am on 1 September 1939, the Polish government requested the promised aid of its allies, France and Britain. The next day, Britain and France issued a joint ultimatum demanding the immediate withdrawal of all German troops from Poland by 12 noon on 3 September 1939.

However, Adolf Hitler did not respond, and, when the ultimatum expired, the two major European powers also formally declared war on Germany.

Fall Weiß

Fall Weiß (Case White), the code name for the Invasion of Poland, was now launched as scheduled. German High Command employed two Army Groups and two Air Fleets.

Army Group North, under Generaloberst Fedor von Bock, comprised the German 3rd and 4th armies. Army Group South, under Colonel Generaloberst Gerd von Rundstedt, consisted of the German 8th, 10th and 14th armies. Together, the two groups had six panzer divisions, four motorised divisions, four light artillery divisions, three mountain divisions and thirty-seven infantry divisions with a total of more than 3,100 armoured vehicles at their disposal.

The German army units were supported by approximately 2,000 aeroplanes, ready for operation, from Air Fleet 1, commanded by General Albert Kesselring, and Air Fleet 4, commanded by General Alexander Löhr.

The German Army had a troop strength of more than 1.6 million, plus the support of three Slovak divisions with about 50,000 men, which supported the Wehrmacht. On the Polish side, there were thirty-seven infantry divisions, two motorised brigades, eleven cavalry brigades, roughly 750 mostly old, small, lightweight armoured fighting vehicles and around 900 planes, most of them of older design.

The plan was for Army Group South to strike from Upper Silesia and proceed in the general direction of Warsaw, while Army Group North advanced eastwards and southwards from East Prussia and Pomerania, executing a pincer movement to enclose the Polish forces.

The Polish reaction

It must be noted at this point that the Polish high command had drawn up no plan of action for the defence of the country in the event of an invasion by the German Wehrmacht. From the outset it expected defeat and a military catastrophe, as its troops were clearly outnumbered and its forces at a severe technical disadvantage.

The objective of the Polish forces was therefore to engage the Wehrmacht troops for as long as possible and to wear them down while retreating to prepared positions until the Allies supported them from the West. Nevertheless, France and Britain hardly undertook any military operations in those weeks, which meant that there was no relief for the Polish Army. The so-called 'Phoney War' on the Western Front began.

The German forces advanced systematically, quickly and as scheduled by Wehrmacht high command.

The greatest concentration of Polish troops was to the west of Warsaw. Here lay the Lodz and Poznan Armies, which were, however, 'overlooked' by German reconnaissance, allowing the German Army Group South to advance unimpeded towards Lublin. These 'forgotten' armies now regrouped and tried to break through the flank of the main thrust of the German advance in order to retreat across the Vistula. There then followed the single largest battle in the Polish Campaign, the Battle of the Bzura.

On the ground, the troops of the Wehrmacht only succeeded in winning control over the Polish cavalry and light armoured vehicles with the help of close air support in the form of Stuka attacks by the Luftwaffe. On 16 September, Army Group South encircled the two Polish armies and bombarded them continuously from the air until they capitulated on 20 September. The entire Polish Western Front collapsed, and the Polish government under Prime Minister Felicjan Slawoj Skladkowski fled into exile in Romania.

After trying in vain to capture Warsaw, which had been surrounded since 9 September, the Luftwaffe also began massive air attacks on the capital city on 26 September 1939. Warsaw capitulated two days later, followed by the last Polish troops on 6 October 1939. Although this is the official end of the Invasion of Poland, Germany and the Soviet Union had already divided up the conquered country between them on 28 September.

Negotiations with Russia

Once again, Joachim von Ribbentrop entered into negotiations with the Soviet government on the future boundaries. Originally, the area west of the Vistula river was to have fallen to the Germans, but Stalin himself suggested extending the area to include Brest-Litovsk. In this way, the Polish population was not divided, thus avoiding pre-programmed unrest.

The German Reich also annexed the Polish territories it had ceded after the First World War and further areas of Central Poland, while Eastern Poland fell to the Soviet Union. The 'Blitzkrieg' against Poland was followed by long years of occupation with cruel and inhuman deportations and frequent violence against the Polish population.

In this first campaign of the Second World War, more than 17,000 German soldiers lost their lives. The number of Polish army personnel killed in action is estimated at 60,000, although more than 690,000 soldiers were taken prisoner by the Germans, which in most cases was the equivalent of a death sentence.

Chapter 1

7th Fliegerdivision (Air Division)

Kurt Student, a veteran pilot from the First World War, shaped the face of the German Fallschirmtruppe more than any other. He played a decisive role in the development, deployment and operational planning of the new unit. As permanent commander-in-chief of the new airborne division, he was not only a father figure and caring superior officer for all his men, but also a legend in his own lifetime. (Janzyk)

The formation and continuous funding of the 7th Fliegerdivision began after the occupation of the Sudetenland in 1938. Prior to this, this still very new and experimental division of the German Wehrmacht was deployed in an uncoordinated manner and followed differing principles, partly under the command of the army and partly under that of the Luftwaffe. In other words, at the same time, there were paratroopers wearing the uniform of the army and others wearing that of the Luftwaffe. As a result, there were two different insignia for the paratroopers within the Wehrmacht, one for army and one for Luftwaffe paratroopers. From March 1938, the parachute infantry battalion, a relatively small army unit formed from the parachute infantry company established on 1 April 1937 in Stendal, the 15th company of the Infanterie-Lehr-Regiment (infantry instruction regiment), was based in the Roselies barracks in Brunswick. It is hardly surprising, however, that this elite unit was dependent on material and infrastructural support from the Luftwaffe. Training courses for paratroopers, for example, were conducted by the training staff of the Luftwaffe and using their planes, at the Fallschirmschule (Parachute School) in Stendal.

German army command saw this new parachute unit as a means to launch surprise attacks in order to capture bridges and other key terrain behind enemy lines, and to establish bridgeheads and hold them while ground troops advanced.

The Luftwaffe, on the other hand, which had already been training soldiers as paratroopers since 1936, at first in the Regiment General Göring in Berlin and later in the 1st Parachute Regiment in Stendal, had different operational principles. The paratroopers of the Regiment General Göring were specifically trained to commit acts of sabotage or carry out commando operations in small groups behind the enemy lines.

As early as late summer 1935, Luftwaffe high command began to draw up its initial plans and ideas for the establishment, deployment and training of paratroopers with the '*Ausbildungskommando Immans*,' named after Captain Friedrich Wilhelm Immans, an

The awarding of the Luftwaffe paratrooper qualification insignia was announced on 16 November 1936 in the Luftwaffenverordnungsblatt. The decree of 10 May 1937 specified the conditions more closely, stating that members of the paratroopers would receive the badge immediately after successfully completing the training course, other soldiers only after a corresponding probationary period. This early non-ferrous metal badge was manufactured by the Wilhelm Deumer company, which was based in Lüdenscheid. (Private collection)

experienced parachutist and one of the founding fathers of the parachute regiment in Germany. In summer 1936, the Luftwaffe established the first military parachute school in Stendal under his command, along with that of Captain Alfred Kuhno and also of former police officer Georg Diete, both also sport parachutists and experts in this field. The first parachute training course was held from 10 August to 26 September 1936. On 5 November 1936, the first Luftwaffe paratrooper qualification insignia, to be worn on the paratrooper's tunic, was awarded.

From early 1939 onwards, however, Hermann Göring succeeded in bringing all Wehrmacht paratroop units under the command of the Luftwaffe, in the 7th Fliegerdivision.

Establishment of 7th Fliegerdivision

The newly created 7th Fliegerdivision, under its first divisional commander, General Kurt Student, was to comprise of three Fallschirmjäger-Regimente (parachute regiments), various divisional troops and air transport units equipped with Ju 52s.

Each regiment had three battalions, each comprising the battalion staff, a signals and engineer platoon and four infantry companies, whereby as a rule, the 4th infantry company, as a support company, was equipped with medium-heavy weapons such as machine guns or light mortars.

By mid-1939, however, Luftwaffe Supreme Command and the 7th Fliegerdivision had succeeded in almost fully establishing Fallschirmjäger Regiment 1 (FJR 1), which took its Battalion I from the companies of General Göring Regiment, which had already received parachute training.

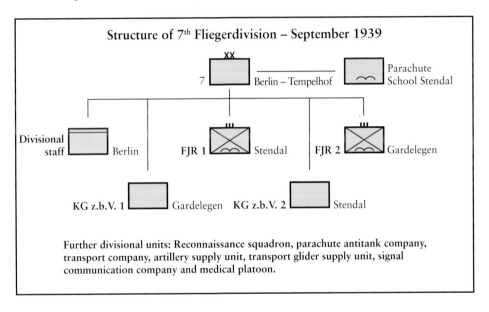

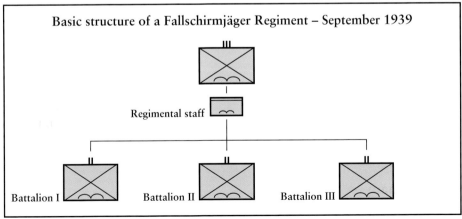

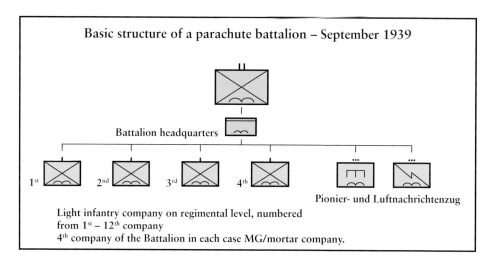

Basic structure of a parachute battalion – September 1939

Battalion headquarters

1st   2nd   3rd   4th   Pionier- und Luftnachrichtenzug

Light infantry company on regimental level, numbered
from 1st – 12th company
4th company of the Battalion in each case MG/mortar company.

The army paratrooper qualification insignia was created on 1 September 1937 and announced in the Heeresverordnungsblatt of 1 July 1938. As a military badge, it was awarded to all ranks together with the jump licence on successful completion of parachute training. In contrast to the Luftwaffe insignia, the wreath here was made solely of oak leaves, and not half of laurel leaves, as was the former. The example shown here is made from aluminium and comes from an early batch manufactured by C.E. Juncker, Berlin. (Private collection)

The army's parachute infantry battalion, which was transferred to the Luftwaffe on 1 January 1939 and also had a strong engineer platoon, formed the Battalion II. Its personnel comprised both older paratroopers transferred from the other two battalions and newly drafted recruits.

7th Fliegerdivision began to establish its Fallschimrjäger Regiment 2 (FJR 2) in early 1939, and by the middle of the year, Battalion I had almost reached target strength at its new base in Gardelegen. However, this was only possible due to the fact that in addition to some experienced paratroopers of the FJR 1, aggressive advertising brought many volunteers from the SA-Standarte 'Feldherrenhalle.' Numerous reservists were also drafted into the companies.

Merkblatt

für den Eintritt als Freiwilliger in das

Fallschirm=Jäger=Rgt. 1 Stendal

Die Einstellung von Freiwilligen in das Fallschirm-Jäger-Rgt. 1 erfolgt am 1. 10. jeden Jahres.

1. Die Dienstzeit beträgt 2 Jahre. Bei entsprechender Eignung zum Unterführer ist eine Weiterverpflichtung auf insgesamt 12 Jahre möglich.

2. Die Uniform des Regiments ist die der Luftwaffe, mit gelber Waffenfarbe und einem hellgrünen Ärmelstreifen mit der Aufschrift »Fallschirm-Jäger-Rgt. 1«. Nach beendeter Fallschirmausbildung erfolgt die Verleihung des Fallschirmschützenabzeichens, das auf der linken Brustseite getragen wird.

3. Es werden Freiwillige vom 17. bis zum vollendeten 22. Lebensjahr eingestellt. Vor der Einstellung werden die Freiwilligen zur Ableistung ihrer Arbeitsdienstpflicht herangezogen.

4. Voraussetzung für die Einstellung ist, daß der Freiwillige

    a) die deutsche Staatsangehörigkeit besitzt,

    b) wehrwürdig ist,

    c) tauglich ist,

    d) daß der Frw. nicht Jude oder jüdischer Mischling ist,

    e) auf Grund eines militärischen Gutachtens fallschirmschützentauglich ist,

    f) nach Ableistung einer psychologischen Eignungsprüfung als Fallschirmschütze geeignet ist,

    g) gerichtlich nicht vorbestraft ist,

    h) unverheiratet ist,

    i) die Gewähr bietet, daß er jederzeit rückhaltlos für den nationalsozialistischen Staat eintritt.

    Die Untersuchungen zu e und f werden von der Dienststelle veranlaßt.

Als Einstellungsunterlagen sind von jedem Bewerber einzureichen:

    a) ein handgeschriebener Lebenslauf,

    b) eine amtlich beglaubigte Einwilligungserklärung des gesetzlichen Vertreters,

    c) 2 Paßbilder in bürgerlicher Kleidung ohne Kopfbedeckung,

    d) ein Freiwilligenschein (bei bereits Gemusterten einen Auszug aus dem Wehrpaß).

Formblätter sind bei den polizeilichen Meldebehörden erhältlich.

Im Lebenslauf muß enthalten sein: Geburtstag, Schulbesuch, Beruf, sportliche Betätigung sowie gegebenenfalls Zugehörigkeit zu einer Gliederung der NSDAP.

Meldeschluß:

1. Für Angehörige der landwirtschaftlichen Bevölkerung (sofern sie ihrer Arbeitsdienstpflicht **noch nicht** genügt haben) am 1. 5. des **vorhergehenden** Jahres,

2. für alle anderen Freiwilligen am 1. 10. des **vorhergehenden** Jahres.

Einstellungsgesuche sind zu richten an:

Fallschirm=Jäger=Rgt. 1, Stendal/Altmark.

Abt.: Einstellung.

11241. 38. HC

This information sheet on service in Fallschirmjäger Regiment 1 was published in 1938 and displayed in the Wehrmeldeämter (army records offices). It describes the criteria a recruit had to meet in order to enlist with the newly formed parachute division. (Janzyk)

In contrast, formation of Battalion II of Fallschirmjäger Regiment 2 did not begin until June 1939 in Tangermünde. Like all other units, it consisted mainly of older, experienced paratroopers, particularly on the top level, and it was not fully formed until mid-1940. The establishment of Fallschirmjäger Regiment 3 did not begin until the middle of 1940.

The first commander and holder of Luftwaffe Fallschirmschützenschein (jump licence) number 1 was Bruno Oswald Bräuer. He served as an NCO in the Prussian army and was promoted to Leutnant in 1919. In 1922, he moved to the Berlin police force. In the course of the years, the paramilitary police unit known as the Polizeigruppe Wecke became the state police force Landespolizeigruppe General Göring and eventually Regiment General Göring, and Bräuer always held top positions in it. When the parachute battalion of the Regiment General Göring was established, he became Battalion Commander. On 24 April 1940, Bräuer was awarded the Knight's Cross of the Iron Cross as regimental commander of Parachute Regiment 1 for service in the invasion of Holland. (Private collection)

The Division had its first public appearance at the parade for the Führer in Berlin on 20 April 1939, which brought a fresh wave of applications with volunteers from all branches of the Wehrmacht.

Order to go into action and mobilisation

On 31 August 1939, under the code name 'Fall Weiß' (Case White), Wehrmacht high command issued the following orders for 7th Fliegerdivision:

'7th Fliegerdivision – reinforced by 16th Infantry Regiment – is the operational reserve on the highest level, and as such, will deploy on D-Day in the Legnica area.'

Group photograph, presumably taken at the end of October/beginning of November 1939, of the officers of FJR 1. On his ribbon bar, Hauptmann Prager is already wearing the Iron Cross awarded to him for service in the Polish campaign. In addition to regimental commander Oberst Bräuer, the photo shows other officers, for example Franz Stangenberg, Rudolf Böhmler, Karl Heinz Becker, Karl Lothar Schulz, Walther Gericke or Harry Hermann. (Private collection)

Luftwaffe high command had already ordered the general mobilisation of the division in advance, on 18 August 1939. However, in contrast to the majority of the Wehrmacht units, the division did not receive its final relocation orders until quite late, which allowed the conclusion that there was definitely no plan to deploy the paratroopers at the start of the Invasion of Poland.

When war broke out on 1 September 1939, 7th Fliegerdivision moved as ordered, reaching the assigned area in the late evening. The battalions were given accommodation near the respective airfields from which they would be operating, while divisional staff was quartered in Wahlstatt.

On 6 August 1939, just twelve days before the general mobilisation of 7th Fliegerdivision, soldiers of Fallschirmjäger Regiment 1 took part in sporting events organised by the Deutsche Arbeitsfront (German Labour Front). This certificate was awarded for competitors in the discipline 'Keulenzielwurf,' in which stick training hand grenades were thrown at a target. (Janzyk)

At the start of the war, 7th Fliegerdivision comprised of the following:

- FJR 1 with three operational battalions
- FJR 2 with a reinforced operational battalion 1st/FJR 2 plus 5th/FJR 2 and 6th/FJR 2)
- A reduced-strength 2nd/FJR 2 was transferred to Luftwaffe Supreme Command
- Divisional units
- 16th Infantry Regiment
- KG z.b.V. 1 – Kampfgeschwader zur besonderen Verwendung (battle wing for special operations) 1
- KG z.b.V. 2 – Kampfgeschwader zur besonderen Verwendung (battle wing for special operations) 2

Infantry Regiment 16 left 7th Fliegerdivision on 12 September 1939, when army high command airlifted it from the staging area near Legnica to Warsaw. Here, army units were engaged in surrounding strong Polish forces, and the OKH (Oberkommando des Heeres – army high command) continued to use the regiment as reinforcements.

Richard Heidrich was commander of the army's parachute infantry battalion until it was transferred to the command of the Luftwaffe. After Hauptmann Fritz Prager took over his post, Heidrich was Ia Op in 7th Fliegerdivision during the Invasion of Poland. In 1943, as commander of FJR 3, he was awarded the Knight's Cross of the Iron Cross for service in Crete. At the end of the war, now a General, he became the 55th recipient of the Knight's Cross with Oak Leaves and Swords. He died in a military hospital in Hamburg-Bergedorf in 1947. (Janzyk)

Stand by to jump

Altogether, Kurt Student's paratroopers were placed on alert three times. During the first alarm, in the Poznan area, they were to support the two major pincer movements of the army units from East Prussia and Silesia by taking the city of Poznan, which had been bypassed by the army and had substantial garrisons. However, due to the amazingly rapid and extremely favourable development of the situation in Poland for the German Wehrmacht, they were not deployed.

The paratroopers were then to take the important major bridge over the Vistula near Pulawy, south-west of Deblin, a fortified city known under Russian rule as Ivangorod. As a key point at which all Polish troops in this area crossed the Vistula, the mission seemed very promising. Moreover, the terrain was almost perfect for an airdrop. The paratroopers of 1st Regiment were already on board the Ju 52 transport aircraft and ready to jump when the operation was cancelled due to the rapid advance of the ground forces.

The last planned deployment for 7th Fliegerdivision was a parachute drop in Galicia with the aim of establishing a bridgehead over the river San, near Jaroslaw, to support and facilitate the rapid advance of List's army. But this mission was also not realised.

The constant uncertainty about a possible deployment of the paratroopers and the resulting physical and mental stress for the soldiers often led to tense relations with the higher levels of leadership. The paratroopers were continually either loading or unloading their planes, an immense logistical and physical effort. Twelve paratroopers were assigned to each Ju 52, and again and again, they had to pack all their weapons, ammunition, rations, explosives and extra equipment into the drop tank known as a '*Waffenabwurfbehälter*,' prepare the container and 'load' it into the plane. And, of course, the material did not remain on the planes after the 'stand down' was given, but had to be removed, unpacked, the weapons and munitions counted and the checks documented. Four of these bulky containers, containing different weapons and equipment depending on the task of the parachute unit in question, fitted on board a Ju 52.

As more and more of the transport aircraft were pulled out and sent on other missions, the paratroopers' hopes of an airdrop shrank.

Backup operations

Nevertheless, Kurt Student did his best to get his men their first operational experience and obtained the approval of the Commander-in-Chief of the Luftwaffe, Hermann Göring, to move his paratroopers to the Pulawy/Deblin area in a motorised convoy (without III./FJR 1). There, they were ordered to carry out backup and clean-up operations against the scattering Polish troops.

This map shows the three missions planned for 7th Fliegerdivision during the Invasion of Poland (Graphics Verhülsdonk, based on: von Roon 2008)

Chapter 2

II./Fallschirmjäger Regiment 1

Hauptmann Fritz Prager receiving the Iron Cross Second Class from divisional commander General Student. (Private collection)

Mobilisation

Following the Polish government's rejection of the Danzig offer on 19 August 1939, a command meeting of 7th Fliegerdivision was called at short notice in Berlin and attended by all key officers and decision-makers. Due to the perceptible tensions between the German Reich and Poland, and the current political situation, the immediate mobilisation of the division and thus of II./Fallschirmjäger Regiment was ordered that same day.

The battalion commenced implementation of the measures at once, and was able to report to the division on 25 August 1939 that it was ready to move. Shortly before 16.30 hours that day, the deployment order from the Luftgaukommando (Air Command) was received at the battalion headquarters in Braunschweig. Just ninety minutes later, the division issued the code word together with the order for Battalion II to mobilise at 05.00 on 26 August. However, just after 22.00, the 7th Fliegerdivision withdrew the code word and thus the order for Captain Fritz Prager's paratroopers to deploy for the time being.

Men of 6th Company preparing and loading the Ju 52 transport aircraft at Schönfeld airfield near Legnica. (Janzyk)

The battalion remained in Braunschweig, on constant alert, until 31 August 1939, engaged in further preparations for a probable air-drop and filling in any gaps in their training. The companies were also able to stock up on weapons and ammunition.

On the last day of August 1939, at 20.30, the division once again issued the code word for the mission, this time with a departure time of 07.30 hours on 1 September 1939. And on the following morning, at 04.45, with the attack on Poland, the Second World War began.

Transfer to the assembly area

II./FJR 1 moved out as scheduled in a motorised convoy, but left half an hour earlier, at 07.00 hours. As ordered, they took the Autobahn from Braunschweig to Burg-Gommern, where they made their first maintenance stop. They refuelled, the drivers and fleet sergeants serviced the vehicles and the com-bat trains of I./FJR 1 and Kampfgeschwader (bomber wing) for special purposes 1 joined the convoy. The first vehicle set off again at 10.30, and the convoy continued its journey via Gommern – Zerbst – Roßlau – Herzberg – Luckau.

There was a second stop, for one hour, about 3 kilometres from Luckau, again in order to refuel. They left Luckau at 17.00 and pro-ceeded via Lübben – Cottbus – Forst – on the Reichautobahn as far as Hagnau – Goldberg – to their destination in Schönfeld, near Legnica, which they reached at around 23.30. Quarters were quickly allocated, and then it was time for the soldiers of II./Fallschirmjäger Regiment 1 to get some rest.

They spent 2 September 1939 carrying out follow-up work on the fully loaded vehicles and unloading them. It seemed as if an airdrop was on the cards, as the battalion had brought its Waffen-abwurfbehälter (drop tanks). The next day, at 06.30, the battalion received the divisional order for an airdrop at some time after 4 September. The global political situation also continued to esca-late, and just a few hours later, Britain and France declared war on the German Reich.

Everyone worked together to 'load' the Ju 52. Note the different tactical markings on the drop tanks and the cargo parachutes on top. (Janzyk)

Originally, the battalion was to be airdropped near Pulawy, the site of the largest and most important bridge over the Vistula river in this area. Their mission was to capture this strategically important target and hold the river crossing open for Reichenau's army.

However, as the army made faster progress than scheduled and was able to take the bridge itself, the aircraft, which were already loaded and ready for action and had been standing on the airfield at Schönfeld-Seifersdorf since 8 September 1939, were unloaded and stood down just five days later. This was due to the fact that the Ju 52 transport planes were needed for the relocation of Infantry Regiment 16 to Lodz on September 13. At 16.00 hours, the planes were back in Schönfeld and preparation began once again. The battalion still expected to be deployed – though no-one knew how or with what objective.

Above: When the drop tank had been locked in position in the drop chute, the impact cap, which was made of thin metal and can be clearly seen in this photograph, was fitted. Its purpose was to cushion the impact when the container landed, to better protect the tank and its contents against possible damage. (Janzyk)

Left: Schönfeld airfield, 3 September 1939. Leutnant Joachim Haedrich, battalion adjutant, samples the food prepared in the field kitchen. (Janzyk)

No airdrop

On 16 September 1939, major restructuring was carried out, and all Kampfgruppen for special purposes were withdrawn from 7th Fliegerdivision. As all the planes were quickly stripped down and had left Schönfeld-Seifersdorf airfield by the early evening, it was clear to everyone, right down to the last paratrooper in the battalion, that there would be no airdrop now. On 19 September 1939, at about 14.30, battalion headquarters received a further divisional order: 'Transfer to the area around Deblin can be expected within the next few days.'

On the very next day, 20 September 1939, at 05.15 am, the motorised convoy to Poland set out – first via the Reichsautobahn as far as Breslau. From there, it proceeded via Öls – Groß Wartenberg – Kempen – Wieruszow – Wielun – Petrikau – Sulejow/Pilliza – Opoczno (Opole) – Radom – to Zwolen, where it arrived at approximately 22.15. II./FJR 1 spent two days there in makeshift quarters, until the trucks moved off again at 06.30 on 22 September, heading for the airfield in Ulez, 18.5 kilometres north-east of Deblin (Ivangorod). However, they had to interrupt their journey for almost two hours

The orderly office of 6th Company is in use, and the Oberjäger seem to be handing out the pay here. (Janzyk)

Above: Leutnant Alex Dick, platoon leader in 6th Company, Fallschirmjäger Regiment 1, and his men enjoying a 'light snack' on the airfield. (Janzyk)

Below: After the transport aircraft had been ordered elsewhere, the vehicle convoy eastward began, passing through territory already conquered by the army units. (Janzyk)

The fighting around Radow was the first battle of encirclement in the Second World War. Following the German invasion, the Polish Prusy Army fell back with six divisions into the loop of the Vistula river near Radow and prepared to defend the city. They were surrounded and suffered a crushing defeat at the hands of strong tank and motorised units of the Wehrmacht, aided by the Luftwaffe. Around 65,000 Polish soldiers were taken prisoner by the Germans. (Janzyk)

in Pulawy, as Wehrmacht engineers were working on the very bridge which had been their jump target some days before.

The primary mission of II./FJR 1 was to secure valuable enemy equipment and transport it behind the Vistula, which had been defined with Russia as the demarcation line. The battalion was also ordered to clear the woods surrounding Ulez of scattered Polish soldiers.

6th Company, under Oberleutnant Franz Stangenberg, began reconnaissance on the afternoon of 22 September 1939 with a reinforced platoon under Leutnant Claus Geyer. Following further deployments as platoon leader in Holland, on Crete and in Russia, Geyer, who was born in Frankfurt (on the Oder), fell on 1 November 1942 in North Africa, having reached the rank of Hauptmann on the staff of the Kampfgruppe von der Heydte (I./FJR Parachute 3).

A drive through the ruined city, which was heavily bombarded from the air. (Janzyk)

The motorised convoy came to a temporary halt on 20 September in Zwolen, where the battalion spent one and a half days. (Janzyk)

Zwolen, too, was marked by the ravages of the war. Note the road sign: "Pulawy 26 km." (Janzyk)

The paratroopers of II./FJR 1 now had some time to take a look around the town and familiarise themselves with the effects of bombs and artillery shells. (Janzyk)

Right: Not every vehicle managed to reach Zwolen under its own steam, for example these 2- or 2.5-ton Mercedes-Benz lorries. (Janzyk)

Below: The men spent two nights in Zwolen before crossing the Vistula and continuing their journey. They slept in makeshift quarters made from tent squares. (Janzyk)

Above: Officers of 6th/FJR 1 enjoying their 'leisure time'. From left to right: Ober-leutnant Franz Stangenberg, Leutnant Alex Dick and Leutnant Claus Geyer. (Janzyk)

Below: The journey continued on 22.9, across the heavily damaged bridge across the Vistula near Pulawy, destination Ulez airfield. (Janzyk)

Above: Near Deblin, the convoy had to make do with temporary pontoons erected by the engineers. (Janzyk)

Below: Ulez airfield – Oberleutnant Stangenberg can be seen in front of the hangar. (Janzyk)

Above: The Polish Army abandoned the airfield in a hurry. The paratroopers had to examine documents and papers looking for important information. (Janzyk)

Left: Soldiers of the 5th/FJR 1 gathered around the radio. The officers seem particularly interested, though it is unfortunately not known what they are listening to. Battalion commander Hauptmann Prager can be seen in the foreground. (Janzyk)

The events in Poland will now be told as described in the platoon leader's combat report dated 21 October 1939:

Report on reconnaissance mission of 1st platoon, 6th Company, on 22.9.39

At shortly before 17.00 on 22.9., 1st Platoon, 6th Company received orders to carry out reconnaissance via Ulez, Nowodwor and in a general northerly direction, under the leadership of the commander of 7th Fliegerdivision. Main objective: to establish whether there is a strong enemy presence near Ulez that poses a threat to the battalion. 1st Platoon was reinforced with a HMG (heavy machine gun) half-platoon for this mission. As a security measure, it was preceded by two motorcycles with sidecars armed with light machine guns and one Solokrad motorcycle to protect the following motor convoy under the command of platoon leader 2. The platoon proceeded via Nowodwor, Grabow, Jakubiaszek, Lipiny. When the first vehicles of the platoon entered Lipiny, there were several Polish soldiers on the main road through the village. They were ordered to halt and surrender.

However, they fled into the nearest houses, presumably intending to arm themselves. We opened fire, whereby one Polish soldier was shot in the stomach and in the left thigh and seriously wounded. The remaining Poles surrendered when we combed the village. Due to a shortage of fuel, we were no longer able to advance towards Wola Gulowska and Adamow. The platoon reached the main Przytoczno-Deblin road via Budziska and Charlejow and proceeded along it to return to the Ulez airfield. Roads which were hardly passable for lorries presented a major difficulty in carrying out our mission, several times forcing us to take a direction contrary to that planned. The platoon brought with it 8 captured Polish soldiers, and there were no losses on our side.

Geyer, Leutnant

A further reconnaissance mission on the following day brought no new insights, and there was no further contact with the enemy. But in the previous days, the battalion staff had received several reports

Left: Oberjäger (NCOs) of 6ᵗʰ/FJR 1being supplied with rations on the Ulez airfield. They are all wearing jump smocks, and the slits through which the paratroopers can remove their knee guards after the drop can be clearly seen in the side seam above the knee of the paratrooper trousers worn by the man on the right. The soldier in the centre of the picture is wearing another piece of special equipment issued to the parachute forces: brown gauntlets. (Janzyk)

Below: On the airfield, the soldiers also seized weapons, ammunition, equipment or fuel. Note that the para-troopers in this photograph are filling fuel from Polish barrels into German ones! (Janzyk)

Right: Leutnant Claus Geyer was platoon leader of 1ˢᵗ platoon, 6ᵗʰ Company. (Janzyk)

Below: Hauptmann Fritz Prager became battalion commander of the II./FJR 1 when the parachute infantry was incorporated into the Luftwaffe. Born in Chemnitz in 1905, he was awarded the Knight's Cross of the Iron Cross on 24 May 1940 for his battalion's part in the taking of the bridges at Moerdijk/Netherlands. Prager died of cancer in December 1940, by that time a Major and commander of II./FJR 3.

from local residents that numerous Polish units were gathering in the woods east of Okrzeja, which represented a considerable threat to Battalion II in the long term. The battalion commander was forced to take action, and after consultation with the commander of 7th Fliegerdivision, decided that Battalion II would surround the woods and take the Polish troops in it prisoner. The combat report of battalion commander Hauptmann Fritz Prager, dated 27 September 1939, describes the events which had taken place three days previously:

Combat report, II./Fallschirmjäger Regiment 1, on the battle which took place near Wola Gulowska on 24.9.39

1.) On 22.9.39, II./FJR 1 relocated to the Ulez airfield on the Deblin-Brest road, 19 km east/north-east of Deblin, on the orders of 7th Fliegerdivision. Its mission was to capture valuable military equipment and to clear the surrounding woods of remaining Polish army troops. The air base is located 9 km in front of the army's security line (Inf.Reg.93) at the crossroads 4 km south-east of Ryki.

2.) Reconnaissance scheduled for the afternoon of 22.9.39 produced the following results:

    1.   Strong Polish forces with vehicles at Lendo (5 km north-east of the air base). An operation to intercept these forces, launched at 17.00 on 22.9.39, failed. The Polish troops had withdrawn

This map shows the battle plan of the battalion commander of II./FJR Parachute 1, on 24.9.39. The map is an original from 1939, with tactical symbols added by the author. (Janzyk)

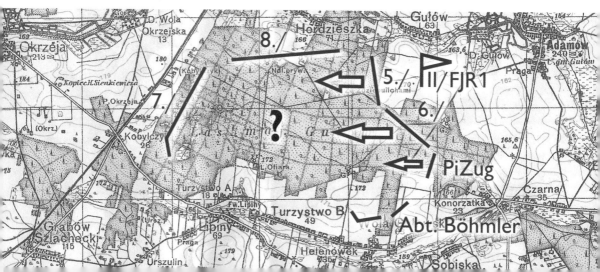

in haste towards the south-east via Welentinow one hour before the battalion arrived. According to concurring statements made by residents who were interrogated separately, these forces comprised 600-800 men with horses and vehicles.

2. Freight train with military equipment at Leopoldow, 8 km north-east of Ryki. The most valuable items were transported to the west bank of the Vistula on eight lorries on the morning of 23.9.

3. The following was ascertained on 23.9, based on the interrogation of inhabitants of the villages north-east of the air base and the statements of Volksdeutsche (ethnic Germans) who arrived here on hearing that German troops were at the Ulez airfield:

3.a. Kilometre-long freight train carrying weapons, ammunition and fuel east of Okrzeja.

3.b. Woods east of Okrzeja apparently rallying point for parts of the Polish army retreating south-east from the direction of Warsaw via Okrzeja and who frequently rearm with weapons taken from the freight wagon located there.

Oberleutnant Rudolf Böhmler, born in Stuttgart in 1914, was already a member of the army's parachute infantry company in Stendal. Following its incorporation into the Luftwaffe, he became a platoon leader in 8th/ FJR 1. At the end of the war, he had reached the rank of Oberst, holder of the Knight's Cross of the Iron Cross and commander of FJR 4. This photograph shows him as an army soldier. On his uniform jacket, he is wearing the officer's dress aiguillette. Above the army paratrooper insignia, there is a Dienstauszeichnungsmedaille (service medal) for 4 years' service, and beneath it, a sport badge. (Janzyk)

3.c. On the afternoon of 23.9, an ethnic German from the German settlement in Jozefow (5 km north-east of Adamow) reported 500 men (artillery and cavalry) in the woods east of Okrzeja. The man, who appeared reliable and is now with the battalion, also reported the presence of some cannons.

3.) The presence of these Polish forces 12 km north-east of the position of Battalion II represented a threat to the safety of our own troops. In carrying out the order to cleanse the surrounding woods, on 24.9., the commander of the 2nd battalion decided to surround the woods east of Okrzeja on three sides and to advance from the east. The Pak (antitank gun) company attached to FJR 1, with infantry equipment, was brought in for this operation. Objectives were to secure the military equipment on the freight train and make it impossible for Poles to obtain further weapons from this source.

4.) To this purpose, the following battalion orders were issued to the leaders of the units on the evening of 23.9.:

1. Enemy forces, approximately 500 men (artillery and cavalry) in the woods 4 km east of Okrzeja.

2. Reinforced Battalion II will surround these woods on the morning of 24.9. and advance from the east.

3. The following will be deployed:

    1. Reinforced 7th Company (Oberleutnant Pagels) and anti-tank gun company (Hauptmann Götzel) will advance via Ryki – Rossosz – Leopoldow station to Grabow. Mission for antitank gun company: to occupy and seal off the woods on the route from Okrzeja to Lipiny. Right wing at western entry to Lipiny, left wing at railway crossing 3 km south-east of Okrzeja.

    2. Reinforced 8th Company (Oberleutnant Pelz) without two infantry squads will advance via Przyoczno – Charlejow – Konorzatka – Adamow – Gulow and seal off the northern edge of the woods on both sides of Hordzieszka.

3. Böhmler detachment (8th Company – 2 infantry squads and one heavy machine gun half-platoon) will branch off to the west in Konorzatka and reach Point 172 (1.5 km northwest of the church in Wola Gulowska)

4. Led by the battalion commander, the main body of the battalion will proceed via Charlejow – Konorzatka – windmill south of Adamow – elevation and terrain to the east, reach Point 170 (1.5 km south of Gulow) and there prepare to attack toward the west. The following will be deployed: on the right, 5th Company (Oberleutnant Herrmann), on the left 6th Company (Oberleutnant Stangenberg), on the left and to the rear of the 6th Company the engineers platoon (Oberleutnant Witzig).

4. A heavy machine gun platoon and 2 mortar units will take up position at Point 170 in such a way that they can protect the advance of the battalion on the woods.

5. Battalion reserve: 2 sections of 8th Company to the east of Point 170

6. Battalion command post: initially at Point 170

7. Communications: with 6th Company via wire, with the rest via radio

8. Aid station: woods, 500 m south of Point 170

9. Commencement of attack: 11.30. On reaching the line of departure, the attacking units will notify 7th Company by firing red-white flares

Departure times from air base 073.0 west – 07.35 north – 08.00 rest

5.) Encirclement of the woods was achieved without problems. Security detachment North was unable to move forward in Konorzatka due to poor road conditions and was bogged down when the battalion arrived there. Members of the detachment had seen unarmed Polish individuals running off towards the west. In Konorzatka, security detachment Böhmler turned off to Wola Gulowska. In an open square in front of the church stood an unarmed Polish captain. Oberleutnant Böhmler took him prisoner and ordered him to get into his vehicle. Suddenly, the Polish officer raised his arm into the air several times. This was a signal, and Böhmler's detachment then came under fire from all sides. They immediately left their vehicles, took cover in the roadside ditch and set up position in the western section of Wola Gulowska. The Polish captain, who had organised the attack on the German troops, was shot. The dust thrown up by the vehicles in the convoy as it approached must have been spotted. Böhmler's detachment suffered heavy losses during the attack: 3 dead and 8 wounded. 2 of the wounded have since died.

6.) At around 9.15, the battalion column, which had reached the position of the Security Detachment North in Konorzatka, heard gunfire, which steadily increased in intensity, from the direction of Wola Gulowska. The battalion commander decided immediately to turn off towards the west with the entire column and approach the assembly area from the south after clarification of the situation in Wola Gulowska. The column reached Wola Gulowska 10 minutes after the attack in the following marching order: Battalion commander – engineers platoon – 5th Company – 8th Company – 6th Company

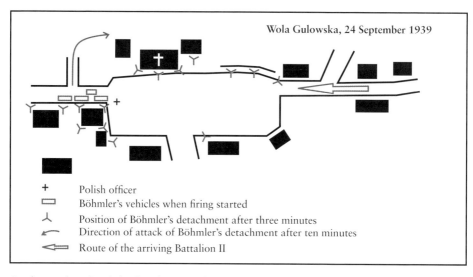

Wola Gulowska, 24 September 1939

+   Polish officer
▭   Böhmler's vehicles when firing started
⅄   Position of Böhmler's detachment after three minutes
↩   Direction of attack of Böhmler's detachment after ten minutes
⇐   Route of the arriving Battalion II

Author's sketch of the battle in Wola Gulowska. (Janzyk)

and came under lively fire from the church steeple and neighbouring houses. By dismounting and seeking cover immediately, they managed to avoid casualties. The ditch near the church and the surrounding farmhouses were cleared. The battalion commander had messengers pass on the following order to the front-most company: 'Front company to dismount immediately, advance to the north past the village, seal off the village.'

The commander of 5th Company, who hurried forward, was ordered to send out a squad to the southern end of the village to secure the route to the south.

The battle for the village was over roughly 15 minutes after the arrival of the battalion. Two further German soldiers were wounded, one of whom later died. Losses on the enemy side in the village: approximately 15 dead, two of them captains, 10 wounded, one of them a captain, 100 prisoners, 60-65 horses, 6-8 vehicles.

This map shows the development of the situation following the battle for the village of Wola Gulowska. (Janzyk)

Above: For many of the young troops, the new combat situation was very confusing. However, the orders from their section and platoon leaders quickly gave them an overview. (Janzyk)

Below: It was already clear at this point that there had been casualties and fatalities. This Hauptgefreiter, deployed as a messenger and mounted on a captured horse, is on his way to the battalion commander. (Janzyk)

Above: These riflemen have climbed down from their lorry and taken cover. (Janzyk)

Below: The first Polish soldiers have been taken prisoner. They are transporting their wounded on a handcart. The third German soldier on the left is worthy of note: he is armed with the Bergmann MP 35, of which only few were used in the Wehrmacht, and is carrying an unusual magazine pouch. (Private collection)

Left: Paratroopers waiting for the command to mount a counter-attack. Two MG 34s can be seen in the ditch. At this early phase of the war, most riflemen were still armed with the Karabiner 98k rifle. The sidecar motorcycle is a BMW R 12. (Janzyk)

Below: The counter-attack has begun, led by 5th and 6th companies. (Janzyk)

The regimental commander (Oberst Bräuer) arrived in the village at the end of the battle. He informed the battalion that Battalion III was on its way to Wola Gulowska. The units of the battalion deployed on the northern edge of the village – one platoon of the 5th and 8th companies and one section of 6th Company then launched an attack towards the north without further orders, with the protection of a heavy machine gun half-platoon, repelled the enemy and captured their train.

Further soldiers surrendered and were brought back to the collecting point, where they were searched for weapons, documents and valuables. (Janzyk)

An Oberjäger of II./FJR 1 searching a Polish soldier. The national insignia of the army can be seen on his steel helmet, identifying him as a veteran of the parachute infantry battalion. (Private collection)

The Polish wounded are recovered by their own troops and initially taken to the temporary military hospital. (Janzyk)

Losses:

German losses:
  2 dead
  6 wounded
Enemy losses:
  43 dead
  25 wounded
  126 prisoners
  102 horses
  6 vehicles

Some enemy troops escaped to the north. III./FJR 1 arrived in Wola Gulowska on motorised vehicles shortly before 12.00. On the orders of the regimental commander, the entire woods were then searched by both battalions from east to west. There was no further engagement with the enemy. Approximately 40 more prisoners were taken.

On 25.9.39., sections of the freight train with military equipment were driven to the railway crossing 2 km south-east of Ryki by

Above: In the background of this photo, the priest of the church in Wola Gulow-ska can be seen. Unfortunately, it is not known what role he played on this day. (Janzyk)

Below: Wounded troops were tended to as quickly as possible by the battalion's medical personnel and Polish civilians. (Private collection)

Above: Oberst Bräuer and his adjutant Graf von der Schulenburg at the battalion aid station hastily set up in the village by Dr. Petritsch. Both German and Polish wounded were treated here. (Janzyk)

Below: A paratrooper guards a captured Polish officer and soldier on the main street in Wola Gulowska. (Private collection)

Right: The battalion surgeon of II./FJR 1 during the Invasion of Poland was Oberarzt Dr. Ludwig Petritsch. As can be seen in this photograph, he had also trained as a paratrooper and was therefore entitled to wear the paratrooper insignia on his uniform jacket. This picture was taken on the train during the return journey from Opole to Braunschweig. (Janzyk)

Below: Oberst Bräuer, the regimental commander, gaining a first-hand impression of the situation in the village of Wola Gulowska. (Janzyk)

Oberst Bruno Bräuer and his men. The paratrooper on the front right is of particular interest, as he is carrying an unusual portable radio set. (Private collection)

members of the battalion and unloaded there. Their contents were transported to the west bank of the Vistula.

Overall losses suffered by the battalion:
  8 dead
  13 wounded

Overall enemy losses:
  58 dead
  35 wounded
  266 prisoners
  167 horses
  12 vehicles with weapons and equipment

Prager, Hauptmann and battalion commander

The battle is over. The two Oberjäger on the right are carrying hand grenade bags around their necks. Two simple canvas bags were connected by a webbing strap at the back of the neck, and each could be loaded with several stick grenades. (Janzyk)

Above: Two paratroopers sitting on a captured wagon. The Luftwaffe eagle can be seen as the national insignia on the steel helmet of the paratrooper in the foreground. The use of this insignia was only discontinued on helmets procured from 1943 onwards, while the black/white/red nationality markings were no longer used from June 1940. (Janzyk)

Below: After the end of the battle, the paratroopers had to search every house and yard in the village. (Janzyk)

Above: Securing the contents of the freight train wagons, mainly rifles and ammunition. (Private collection)

Below: The train was also carrying raw materials such as timber and metals. (Private collection)

Above: The station of Zajezierze, south of Wola Gulowska. (Private collection)

Below: The coffins are carried into the fort. Hauptmann Prager can be identified via his badge of rank. The soldier with the camera is Feldwebel Helmut Wenzel from the engineer platoon Witzig. (Janzyk)

First funerals
The fallen of II Battalion are laid to rest in the fortress of Ivangorod in the General Bema Fort at 12.00 on 26 June 1939. The ceremony was attended by the divisional and battalion commanders.

Above: Three paratroopers from II./FJR 1 pay their last respects to their fallen comrades. (Janzyk)

Below: General Student inspecting the assembled troops. He is still wearing the type of helmet worn in the First World War. It is easily identifiable with its large vent lugs. (Private collection)

Above: The guard of honour fires a salute (Janzyk)

Below: Burial of the first paratroopers from the young German parachute forces killed in action. (Janzyk)

Oberjäger Hans Morcinek from Gleiwitz served in the battalion staff. He died at the age of only 26. (Janzyk)

However, Polish statistics on the battle of 24 September 1939 contradict those of the Germans. The 2nd Battalion of the 1st PAC (1. Pulk Artylerii Ciezkiej), a powerful heavy artillery regiment of the Polish army which was moving towards the west, was deployed in the area east of Wola Gulowska. When the battle was over, German reports speak of 58 dead Polish soldiers.

Yet there are only a total of eleven fallen Polish soldiers buried during this time in the Polish cemeteries around Wola Gulowska. They have been confirmed by Polish sources as artillerymen, among them two captains. Polish figures quote thirty wounded, among them the seriously wounded battalion commander of the II/1st PAC, Hauptmann Zbigniew Boleslaw Mokrzycki, who was taken prisoner and died of his wounds on 27 September 1939, and a further 140 Polish prisoners of war. Unfortunately, it is no longer possible to determine which figures are correct. There are very few data from the Polish side, as the army was in the process of disbanding and personnel lists were no longer being kept. This is true not only in the case of this battle, but for the entire Polish Campaign.

Feldwebel Kurt Mensch from 5th Company died on 24 September 1939, not in battle, but as the result of an accident with his MP 38. On the return journey from Wola Gulowska, the lorry on which he was travelling was jolted when it hit a pot-hole or some similar obstruction. Mensch was holding his machine gun between his legs with the muzzle pointing upwards when it went off. This well-known problem with blowback-operated weapons was first remedied with the help of a leather harness, until the cocking lever was modified so that the bolt was locked forward, preventing inadvertent discharge. (Janzyk)

Former Standarte Feldherrenhalle member Obergefreiter Hans Lorenz of 8./FJR 1 was one of the first German paratroopers killed in action in the Second World War.

Right: Lorenz was buried with his seven other comrades from II./FJR 1 in Fort Iwangorod on 26 June 1939. His parents later received pictures of the cemetery and a letter from the battalion commander, Hauptmann Prager.

Below: Heinrich Blum was in the same company as Hans Lorenz. He was also killed in action during the fighting in Wola Gulowska village.

Left: This propeller, probably from a Polish plane, was erected as a memorial in the first cemetery of the German Fallschirmjägertruppe. It bears the inscription '24.9.39 – Fallen in battle at Wola Gulowska.' (Janzyk)

Below: The cemetery of II./FJR 1 in the fort after the ceremony.

Above: The companies of Battalion II spent the period from 28 September to 5 October in quarters in the Radomsko area. This photo shows the quarters of 6th Company in Ulesie. (Janzyk)

Below: Paratroopers of 6th/FJR 1 performing their ablutions in Ulesie. (Janzyk)

'Farewell Poland ! – Mitropa buffet car Warsaw-Braunschweig-Paris?' The troops have made themselves comfortable on the bed of a Mercedes L3000 lorry, on which they have written these words – typical soldiers' humour. (Janzyk)

Redeployment

Redeployment of 7th Fliegerdivision via Czestochowa to the Radomsko area, where the companies were housed in temporary quarters until 5 October, began on 28 September 1939. The battalion staff, engineer platoon and 5th Company were quartered in Koniecpol, 7th Company in Koniecpol-Stary, 6th Company in Ulesie and 8th Company in Przyrow.

A regimental order dated 3 October 1939 scheduled the final redeployment of the battalion for 5 October at 09.30. Their interim destination was Opole, where the entire division gathered and was accommodated until 10 October. Battalion II was assigned quarters in the Schlesische Portland Zementfabrik (Silesian Portland cement works). Baggage loading began in Opole station on 9 October, and the train departed for Braunschweig as scheduled at 10.00 on the following day. Redeployment of the battalion train in a motorised convoy took place simultaneously.

On 11 October 1939, at around 09.00, Battalion II arrived back at its peacetime barracks in Braunschweig after an absence of over one month and without its fallen and wounded comrades. In recognition of their mission, thirteen Iron Crosses Second Class were awarded to members of II./FJR 1.

Presumably, the eight fallen paratroopers were awarded this medal for bravery posthumously. Moreover, the entire battalion was granted furlough from 13 to 17 October.

Finally, for the sake of completeness, it must be added that two of the battalion's severely wounded died as a result of their injuries in a military hospital in November and December 1939. A further nine paratroopers were discharged, as their wounds meant they were no longer fit for military service. A verified list of the German and Polish fallen and wounded can be found in the Appendix.

General Student salutes as he inspects the ranks of paratroopers assembled to receive the Iron Cross Second Class. (Private collection)

Above: General Student and officers of Battalion II in front of the hangars at Braunschweig air base. (Private collection)

Below: II./FJR 1 marching out after roll call on Braunschweig-Broitzem airfield, led by Hauptmann Prager. (Private collection)

The soldiers of II./FJR 1 – photographs and documents

The following photographs show members of II./Fallschirmjäger Regiment 1. As these pictures were not taken during the Invasion of Poland, they are included as an Appendix to this chapter, together with rare documents, for example excerpts from service record books, jump licences and award certificates.

Above: This group photo was taken in the late summer of 1939. It shows the officers of 5th Company, Fallschirmjäger Regiment 1, who were deployed at Wola-Gulowska. Of particular interest here are the early paratrooper tunics without national insignia and pockets. (Private collection)

Right: In Braunschweig, the home base of II./FJR 1, portrait photos commemorating those who fell during the Polish mission were put on display. In this photograph, Hans Mordhorst, 5th Company, is on duty as guard of honour. (Janzyk)

Hans Mordhorst was a member of 5th Company, Fallschirmjäger Regiment 1, during the Invasion of Poland. He later fought in Holland, in Crete, in Russia and in Africa, before being taken prisoner by the Americans in the West in 1945. This recoloured portrait shows Mordhorst as a Feldwebel. On his paratrooper's uniform tunic, he is wearing the Iron Cross First Class above the Erdkampfabzeichen (Ground Assault Badge) of the Luftwaffe and the army paratrooper qualification insignia. Below them, he is also wearing a black Verwundetenabzeichen (Wound Badge). (Janzyk)

Fritz Räbiger (6th/FJR 1), who only sustained minor injuries in the battle at Wola Gulowska, fell in August 1943 in Sicily, having reached the rank of Oberfeldwebel in FJR 3. This photograph was taken before March 1938, i.e. during his time in the parachute infantry company, as he is wearing the old, pointed epaulettes with the Gothic 'L' of the Infanterielehrregiment (infantry instruction regiment) and the uniform buttons of the 15th Company. (Janzyk)

Ewald Hermann Nickel, here as an Obergefreiter, saw action with 8th Company in Poland. Like almost 90 per cent of Battalion II, he formerly served in the army and is therefore wearing its paratrooper insignia. Above it, the ribbon bar of the 'Medaille zur Erinnerung an den 1. Oktober 1938' (1 October 1938 Commemorative Medal, also known as the Sudetenland Medal) can be seen. (Janzyk)

Otto Schmitt was a member of 7th Company during the Invasion of Poland. He fell just six months later at Moerdijk in Holland. In this photograph he has the rank of Ober-jäger and is wearing the Schützenschnur (Badge of Marksmanship), Level 5. (Janzyk)

Schmitt's grave in Moerdijk, Holland. (Janzyk)

Leutnant Rudolf Witzig in the summer of 1939. One year later, he and his engineer platoon landed at the Belgian fortress of Eben Emael using transport gliders and, carrying shaped charges, which were used for the first time here, making an important contribution to the neutralisation and subsequent capitulation of the fortress. (Janzyk)

Rudolf Witzig, who became known for his participation in the storming of the Belgian fortress of Eben Emael, also saw action in the battle of Wola Gulowska with his engineer platoon. It was here that he suffered the loss of his first paratrooper engineer. This photo shows him as a Leutnant of the army with the parachute infantry. (Janzyk)

üge, mobile Verwendung, Teilnahme an sonstigen tischen Unternehmungen und Kampfhandlungen Verwundungen und ihnen gleichzuachtende Kriegsdienstbeschädigungen	Auszeichnungen	Anerkannt	
		Datum	Unterschrift
ternehmen "Österreich"	S.A. Sportabzeichen		
" "Böhmen-Mähren"	H.J. " "		
?.-14.lo.39 Einsatz-Polen	Fallsch.-Schtz.		
.9.39 Gefecht b. Wola -	Abzeichen		
Gulowska	Eisernes Kreuz		
.-31.5.1940 Einsatz-Holland	II.u.I.Kl. 23.5.40		
.-16.5.40 Gefecht bei			
erdijck-Brücken nach Fallsch.			
sprung.			
(II./Fallsch.-Jg.-Rgt. 1)		13.9.40	
.ftlandeoperation Kreta v.20.5. s 27.5.41 Kämpfe bei Chania .lemes und an der Sudabucht. 10.bis 17.11.41 Kämpfe an der >wehrfront Leningrad.Verwundet ..29.10.41 -Granatsplitter re. 'm. (II./Fallsch.J.Rgt.3)).3.bis 1.10.42 Sicherung im :setzten Gebiet im Bereich des :1.Kdos.3 bei II./F.J.Rgt.3	Verwundetenabzeichen in Schwarz:10.1.42 Luftw.Erdkampfabz. 1.10.42	*Rudolf Rennecke*	

The battle at Wola Gulowska is listed in the Personalstammblatt (personnel data sheet) of the later Oberstleutnant and holder of the Knight's Cross of the Iron Cross with Oak Leaves Rudolf Rennecke. In September 1939, he saw action as an Oberjäger in 6th Company. In the photograph, he is already a Leutnant. (Janzyk)

Rudolf Rennecke after the Crete mission, as Regimentsadjutant (adjutant to the regimental commander), FJR 3. He is wearing a third-model paratrooper's tunic, identifiable by the striking covered zips. The printed camouflage pattern was originally the same splinter-pattern camouflage as that used for the tent square, but was later modified to sand-coloured camouflage or swamp camouflage. (Janzyk)

Alfred Schwarzmann served during the Invasion of Poland as Zugführer in 8th Company of Fallschirmjäger Regiment 1. For the Holland campaign, during which he narrowly escaped death, with the rank of Hauptmann, he was awarded the Knight's Cross of the Iron Cross. He was the winner of three gold medals in gymnastics at the 1936 Olympics. (Janzyk)

Fallschirmschützenschein

Nr. *864*

für *Heeressportlehrer Alfred Schwarzmann*
(Dienstgrad, Vor- und Zuname)

geboren *23. März 19.. zu Fürth / Bay.*

Diensteintritt: *1. 4. 1933*

Truppenteil: *13. J. R. 21*

Inhaber ist befördert:

am: *1. 10. 1934*

zum: *Gefreiten*

am: *1. 5. 1935*

zum: *Unteroffizier*

am: *1. 8. 1936*

zum: *Leutnant*

Schwarzmann
(Eigenhändige Unterschrift)

II. / Fallsch.-Jg.-Rgt. 1
(Ausstellende Dienststelle)

Braunschweig, den *18. Januar* 193*9*
(Ort) (Datum)

Alfred Schwarzmann's jump licence. His rank is entered as Heeressportlehrer (army sports instructor). Hauptmann Fritz Prager brought this winner of several Olympic medals to the parachute infantry with the aim of improving sport instruction and thereby reducing the risk of injury on landing during a parachute drop. (Private collection)

Hauptmann Prager and Oberleutnant Böhmler in Braunschweig, New Year's Eve 1939. They are both wearing the Iron Cross Second Class, awarded for service during the Invasion of Poland, on their ribbon bars. (Janzyk)

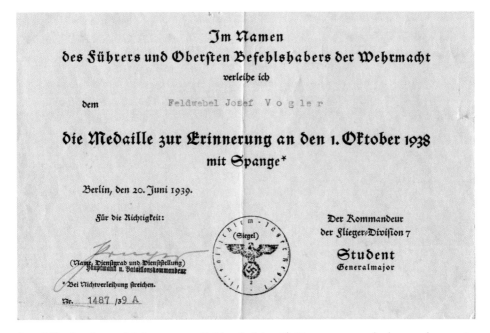

Josef Vogler from Mainz was a Feldwebel in 6th Company and also took part in the battle at Wola Gulowska. One year previously, still a member of the parachute infantry, he had taken part in the occupation of the Sudetenland. This certificate was signed by battalion commander Hauptmann Prager. (Janzyk)

Eduard Baltrock, born in Riga, was a member of the parachute infantry company in Stendal from its founding. He served in Infantry Regiment 33 and volunteered for the army's newly-founded parachute corps. (Private collection)

21

Wehrdienst

Ausbildung

Sonstige Ausbildung, Lehrgänge

Fallschirmschützenausbildung 12.4. – 4.6.1937
Pionierausbildung W.K.F. Kl. 1
Sport Kurs nö Döbersdorf 6.6.12. – 17.12.1937
Hilfslehrer-Ausbildung 6.10.1. – 4.3.1938

Abzeichen usw.

Fallschirmschützen – Abzeichen Heer 1.9.1937

Eduard Baltrock received his army paratrooper qualification insignia on 1 September 1937, roughly three months after successfully completing the training course. (Private collection)

A. Zuletzt zuständige Wehrersatzdienststelle: ....

Braunschweig

B. Truppenteil bzw. Dienststelle:[1]

von	bis	Truppenteil bzw. Dienststelle	Staffel usw.	Nr. der Stammrolle
4.1.39		*F. J. R. 1*	*6. Kp.*	*22*
1.7.40		*F. J. R. 3*	*5. Kp.*	
		~~*2. Balln. Jg. Erl. Batl.*~~		
16.14.		*Fl. H. Abt. A(o) 6/III*	*Disonio Jauban*	
		Lw.- Fausnhain *J. Jl. Müllfund*		
6.4.45		*Fl. H. Flak A(o) 12 =*	*Dessau Kochraboff*	

C.

Jetzt zuständiger Ersatztruppenteil	Standort
~~*Flg. Ausb. Regt. 42*~~	~~*Salzwedel*~~
~~*Fallsch. Jg. Ersatz- Batl.*~~	~~*Stendal/Swm*~~
~~*Fallsch. Jg. Ers. Batl.*~~	~~*Stendal*~~
~~*Fallsch Jäg Jg Btl. 2*~~	~~*Fahlberg*~~

(Meldung dortselbst nach Rückkehr vom Truppenteil bzw. Dienststelle oder Lazarett, zuständig für Ersatz an Bekleidung und Ausrüstung)

[1] Vom Truppenteil bzw. Dienststelle einzutragen und bei Versetzungen von einem zum anderen Truppenteil bzw. Dienststelle derart abzuändern, daß die alten Angaben nur durchstrichen werden, also leserlich bleiben.

Weiterer Raum für Eintragungen auf Seite 17.

4

The fourth page of a soldier's pay book usually shows to which military unit he belongs. Baltrock's pay book states that during the Invasion of Poland, he served in 6th Company, Fallschirmjäger Regiment 1. Members of the forces carried their pay book with them while on active service.

The corresponding page in the Wehrpass (service record book) is page 12, but also includes Baltrock's period of service in the parachute infantry. The service record book was kept by the unit during active service and only handed over to the soldier when he retired from the service. (Private collection)

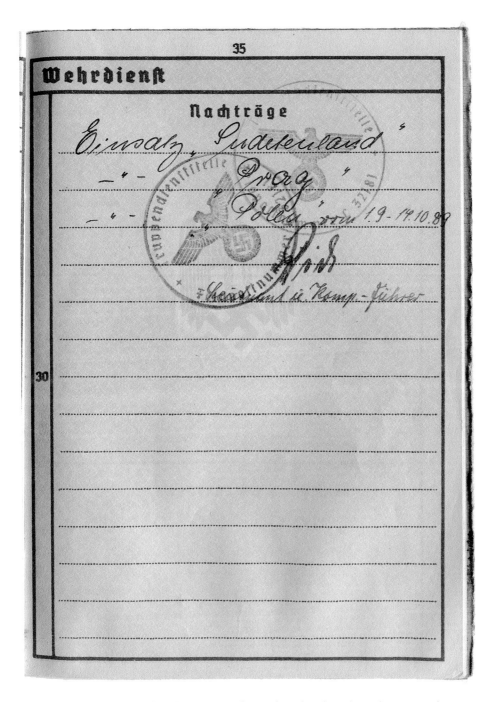

An entry on page 35 also documents that Eduard Baltrock took part in the Invasion of Poland. He survived the war. (Private collection)

Left: This passport photo from Baltrock's pay book shows him as an Oberfeldwebel of the Luftwaffe. (Private collection)

Below: Baltrock not only took part in the battle at Wola Gulowska, but in a total of three parachute drops during the war. The last, in Sicily, cost him his right arm. (Private collection)

III./Fallschirmjäger Regiment 1

General Student has just awarded Oberstleutnant Sydow the Knight's Cross of the Iron Cross Second Class. The stripe of the 'FallschirmJäger Regiment 1' is clearly visible on the sleeve of Sydow's uniform jacket. Sydow left the parachute unit that same year. Student is wearing the 2ⁿᵈ model 'Flieger-Generalsdegen' (Luftwaffe officer's sword), which was introduced in 1938. The sword had been awarded to Luftwaffe generals by Göring himself since 1935. However, Student is actually contravening a regulation issued in June 1939 by wearing the sword with a waist belt and crossbelt here. (Janzyk)

Mobilisation

Like Battalion II, Battalion III was placed on the alert and mobilized by order of 7th Fliegerdivision on 19 August 1939. On 1 September 1939, it moved in a vehicle convoy as scheduled, as did all other divisions, to its assigned operational air base at Aslau near Legnica, and was quartered in Lichtenwaldau. On arrival, the Ju 52s were prepared and equipped for a possible parachute mission. The drop tanks were packed with weapons, explosives and supplies, the troops loaded up with ammunition and waited for the order to go ahead, which was not issued until 12 September.

Protection of the command post

On the morning of 13 September, in Sucha, Battalion III was placed under the command of Luftwaffe General Wolfram von Richthofen. The General had requested a parachute battalion as support in protecting his command post, which he had transferred to a position near the Sucha estate on the river Pilica in eastern Poland.

On 12 September, Battalion III was transported by air, in haste and without its train, from Aslau to Radom. On arrival, the planes were hurriedly unloaded, and the units gathered in their assigned locations. They only set up camp for one night, as the battalion was to advance the next morning with the help of lorries borrowed from Stuka squadron 77, to a position at Sucha-Kamien. The commander of Battalion III FJR 1, Oberstleutnant Otto Sydow, contacted the air force commander for special operations, von Richthofen, who assigned him the task of securing the command post and airfield at Sucha-Kamien with combat outposts. As reconnaissance had revealed scattered enemy forces south of the Pilica river, approximately 30 km away, their main focus was to the west.

Oberstleutnant Sydow immediately flew over the area in a Fieseler Fi 156 Storch, the standard liaison aircraft of the Wehrmacht, in order to define possible locations for outguard posts and pass on his suggestions to General von Richthofen. The Fi 156 Storch had extremely good slow speed capabilities and was able to take off and land using very short airstrips, which made it ideal for

Above: The Ju 52 transport planes of the 3rd group of the Kampfgeschwader (bomber wing) for special operations 1 stand ready and waiting for the deployment of Battalion III on the front-line airfield Aslau. The wing consisted of 4 Groups, each with 4 squadrons. (Janzyk)

Below: The field kitchen staff of 11th Company 'in position' in Lichtenwaldau. (Janzyk)

Left: A souvenir snapshot taken during the flight to Radom. (Janzyk)

Below: This original map shows the operational area of Battalion III./FJR 1 around the Sucha estate. (Janzyk)

reconnaissance flights. Von Richthofen approved Sydow's proposals, and by late afternoon on 13 September, the companies had taken up their positions and the paratroopers were able to set up preliminary fortifications and radio links.

In the course of that afternoon, an officer from another airborne unit reported to the air force commander for special operations that he had sighted a Polish squadron in the Kostrzyn area while flying over the front line. Battalion III therefore received orders, at around 20.00 hours, to carry out reconnaissance in the Bialobrsegi – Wysnierzyge – Sukonno – Jedlinsk area on the following morning. Their objective was to ascertain

The order to move to Radom finally arrived. This photo shows men of 10th Company during the flight to Poland. The Gefreiter in the foreground is sitting at an MG 15, which was used in many Luftwaffe planes as defence against enemy aircraft. (Janzyk)

whether there were Polish forces in this area, and if so, where. To carry out its mission, Battalion III, which was without its own combat train, was supplied with four 2-cm anti-aircraft guns, four command jeeps and nine lorries, which arrived at 07.30.

At the same time, Oberstleutnant Sydow issued the following orders to the commanders of the four companies:

1. Enemy forces in the woods south of the Pilica, 20 to 30 km west of Sucha, strength unknown. Polish squadron sighted by an officer of another unit in the Kostrzyn area on 13.9.
2. The battalion's mission is to carry out reconnaissance in the above-mentioned area and capture any scattered Polish troops in the villages and woods there.

On arrival at Radom airfield, the planes were unloaded, and the men assembled by company. This photograph shows the assembly area of 11th/FJR 1. Company commander Oberleutnant Karl-Heinz Becker is already present. Note the soldier kneeling on the left. He has just connected two belt boxes for the MG 34 with a field bag strap in order to be able to carry them more easily around his neck. In the background, you can see a field hangar in mid-construction. (Janzyk)

3. The mission will be carried out by three assembled units in platoon strength, each supported by an anti-aircraft gun and a portable-radio section, under the command of the respective company commanders. I myself will be in charge of the middle column. The march route for the column and breaks for the establishment of communications have already been defined.

4. A further objective is to capture escaped Polish soldiers hiding in the villages in civilian clothing. Exact details of procedure have been discussed with the company commanders.

5. Air reconnaissance by Leutnant Wagler in a Fieseler Storch

Sydow, Oberstleutnant and battalion commander

First contact with the enemy

During the briefing, Oberleutnant Werner Dunz, commander of 10th Company, reported that one of his outguard sentries had heard the sound of vehicles near Stawiszyn. As a result, the column of 9th and 10th companies was instructed to search the woods between Jasionna and Stawiszyn from the north and the south respectively.

At 09.30, the first units of 10th Company began to leave their outguard positions and advance. After almost 100 metres, in front of

The paratroopers of Battalion III./FJR 1 await further orders. (Private collection)

In the meantime, the destroyed planes are inspected and first souvenirs taken. The national insignia has been cut out of the tail unit of the plane behind PZL P23B-Karas. (Janzyk)

the southern edge of the woods, between Jasionna and Stawiszyn, Dunz's commando came under heavy machine gun and rifle fire, whereupon some parts of the commando withdrew without waiting for corresponding orders.

When the battalion commander arrived at this position, he reported that Polish soldiers to the left and right of the path leading out of the woods at a distance of about 100 metres had surrendered after Oberstleutnant Dunz opened fire. Just a few seconds later, the enemy again opened fire on parts of 10th Company from the woods with rifles and machine guns, seriously wounding Oberstleutnant Dunz. His radio operator and close-in guard, an Oberjäger, were killed, which meant that the radio equipment was also out of operation.

In this early, initial combat phase in the history of the German parachute units, seven paratroopers fell. In addition, five paratroopers were seriously wounded, only three of whom, including company commander Oberstleutnant Dunz, were recovered in the course of the battle.

Above: The company commander, too, has to wait for further instructions. Ober-stleutnant Becker, commander of 11th Company, with his 'Spieß' (top sergeant), Oberfeldwebel Plomann (on the right next to Becker). (Janzyk)

Below: Almost all the Polish aircraft destroyed on the ground and no longer fit for action were outdated planes like these double-deckers of type PWS 26 or Poli Karpov U-2LNB, (Janzyk)

Under covering fire from the 2-cm anti-aircraft gun, the unit withdrew to the village of Stawiszyn, but came under fire here, too. Meanwhile, a sniper in a tree was quickly spotted and eliminated. Dunz's detachment secured the perimeter of the village and waited for the rest of 10th Company, which was to follow up immediately on the orders of the battalion commander. As Oberleutnant Dunz was seriously wounded, Oberleutnant Adolf Specht, platoon leader of 10th Company, took command of the company in the meantime.

Leutnant Wagler, who was flying reconnaissance over the combat area in the Fieseler Storch, continued to report that the enemy held the forest between Jasionna and Stawiszyn. From his plane, which was able to fly at a reduced flying speed of approximately 45 km/h, he also saw the unit of 9th Company, led by Oberleutnant Otto Gessner, which was approaching Jasionna from the north, come under fire from the village.

Wagler was forced to break off his reconnaissance flight when he, too, came under fire. He was unable to determine the precise strength of the Polish forces.

Luftwaffe, Hermann Göring, also arrived at the Radom airfield. In this photograph, an unidentified Oberstleutnant is briefing him on the task force's transport planes. (Janzyk)

On receiving orders to relocate to the Sucha estate, the men immediately set out on lorries borrowed from the Stuka squadron. The effects of the war were clearly visible in the villages and towns, too, and this wrecked model B or C Panzerkampfwagen IV is evidence of determined defence efforts by the Polish forces. (Janzyk)

Based on these events, the battalion commander decided to bring in further units of the battalion and surround the enemy in the woods. In substance, his orders were as follows:

1. Capture the village of Jasionna and seal it off to the south.
2. Form a platoon comprising the remaining troops in Sucha, under the command of Leutnant Wagler, with orders to push forward into the Dembniak area from the north via Jasionna and seal off the woods in the northwest.
3. Two platoons of 11th Company, under company commander Karl-Heinz Becker, to leave the outguard posts on the main road to Warsaw and advance via Sucha – Stawiszyn – Branica to the Branica – Dembniak road and contact Wagler's platoon there. On command, they will later advance into the western edge of the woods from the west.

Together with Ernst Udet, Göring takes stock of the situation in person. At this point, the men of 11th Company FJR 1 are still on the air base. (Janzyk)

In addition, the outguard of 9th Company, which was now in position at the Sucha-Korzen stream crossing, was reinforced by a heavy machine-gun platoon from the Sucha estate. It was ordered to insert itself between the units at Suskimanek and Jasionna and establish contact with the neighbouring units.

Above: Members of 11th Company come into contact with the civilian population during a brief halt. (Janzyk)

Below: The command post of the air force commander for special operations was set up in the main building of the Sucha estate. (Private collection)

Above: Paratroopers from 9th Company are issued their rations immediately prior to taking up their securing positions. The mobile field kitchen is mounted on the bed of a lorry. (Private collection)

Below: Preparations for the establishment of outguard posts are now underway, with all available equipment and munition being brought in. (Private collection)

Support from heavy weaponry

At around 11.30, the battalion commander presented his plan of action to the air force commander for special operations in Sucha and requested that combat planes should bomb the woods to "soften up" the enemy forces in preparation for the attack of Battalion III.

At this point, Oberstleutnant Sydow was already proceeding from the assumption that they would find an extremely well-armed and strong enemy presence in the woods. However, the battalion commander's request was refused. Instead, Battalion III was assigned an 8.8-cm anti-aircraft battery which was in position near the Chuscischow estate to protect the Sucha-Kamien airfield and was now brought forward on the orders of Oberstleutnant Sydow to a position 1 km east of the road leading out of Stawiszyn to the south. The firing distance from here to the forest was now approximately 3 km. The 8.8-cm anti-aircraft battery opened fire at around 14.00, while the fighter planes fired on the edges of the woods with machine guns. After firing 200 shots, the entire ammunition of the battery, 10th Company, 1st Platoon from 9th Company under Leutnant Horst Trebes, and Wagler's combined platoon advanced on the woods from the south and north. However, it quickly became evident that the artillery fire had hardly hit the enemy forces effectively. Reconnaissance patrols from 10th Company, who recovered wounded troops holding out on the edge of the woods, discovered that the enemy had established defence positions on both their southern and northern edges. The reconnaissance patrols immediately encountered heavy machine gun and mortar fire from these positions, and the battalion commander decided to halt the attack and order the companies to return to their former positions.

As Leutnant Wagler reported that there were fewer enemy troops on the western edge of the woods, Oberstleutnant Sydow again contacted the air force commander for special operations on the afternoon of 14 September, but was only able to speak to his second-in-command, General von Stutterheim.

The men of 9th Company set out for their assigned positions. Due to a shortage of vehicles, a 'shuttle service' was set up, here using a jeep of type Wanderer W11, which had a 3-litre straight-six cylinder engine with 60 PS (approx. 59.18 hp). (Private collection)

To the relief of the commander of III./FJR 1, General von Stutterheim immediately promised the support of fighter planes, and a massive assault on the woods was scheduled for 17.45. Due to the risk of injury from bombs and flying shrapnel, some advance units of the battalion had to be pulled back.

17.15 hours: Two platoons from 11th Company, led by the company commander, arrive in the village of Stawiszyn and are briefed on the position and their mission by the commander using a map.

17.30 hours: The noise of battle is heard from the tiny village of Branica. 11th Company advances on the village. Taking the village, it advances further on the Branica – Dombniak road. Company losses: 2 wounded. Polish losses: 6 dead, 5 wounded, 17 prisoners. 11th Company remains under heavy fire from the woods 1 km north-west and 2 km west of Branica.

Private Erich Lotzn was an MG 2 machine gunner in 11th Company. Many of the photographs in this book are from his private photo album. This portrait photograph was taken on 27 November 1939. (Janzyk)

17.40 hours: Two flights of fighter planes open fire on the edges of the woods between Jasionna and Stawiszyn.

17.45 hours: No fighter plane attack on the woods between Jasionna and Stawiszyn. Instead, the pilots bombard the woods near Smardzew, much further to the south. They come under heavy machine-gun and rifle fire over Branica. This proves conclusively that there were strong Polish forces not only in the woods near Jasionna, but also near Branica.

Withdrawal to outguard positions

Once again, the battalion commander had not been able to realise his plan. At nightfall, all units of Battalion III were ordered to withdraw for the time being to the outguard positions they had been assigned on 13 September to carry out their core mission; the protection of the air base.

On the evening of 14 September, Oberleutnant Adolf Specht, the officer in charge of 10th Company, which was currently located in Stawiszyn, received the following orders:

> 10th Company will send out reconnaissance patrols to re-establish connection with 11th Company, bring the entire company back to Stawiszyn and secure the village from all sides until the dead and wounded of 10th Company have been recovered from the edge of the woods. I then intend to withdraw all battalion forces from Stawiszyn.
>
> Sydow, Oberstleutnant and battalion commander

After issuing these orders, the commander of Battalion III returned to the air force command post at Sucha to make arrangements for the subsequent supply of ammunition and rations during the night. Via an already-laid field line, which established communication through telephone lines, the commander of 11th Company, Oberleutnant Becker, reported that his company was engaged in combat with enemy forces in Branica. Oberstleutnant Sydow ordered them to evacuate their position in Stawiszyn and form an oblique defence line to the east of the village, supported by 9th Company. General von Richthofen strongly disapproved of this decision and ordered the battalion commander to leave 10th and 11th companies in position in Stawiszyn as covering units. Oberstleutnant Sydow protested and again emphasised the reasons for his decision, but General von Richtofen insisted, and Battalion III was therefore obliged to carry out his orders.

At approximately 23.40, loud sounds of battle were once again heard from the Stawiszyn area. About one hour later, the commander of 11th Company himself arrived in Sucha and reported to the battalion commander that the positions of 10th and 11th companies around the village of Stawiszyn were under systematic, simultaneous and coordinated attack by Polish forces from the north, west and south. According to information from prisoners taken by the Germans, enemy strength was at least one and a half regiments.

The commander of 11th Company, Oberleutnant Karl-Heinz Becker, was also awarded the Iron Cross. Later, he was decorated with the Knight's Cross of the Iron Cross for service in Crete in 1941, and in 1945, as commander of FJR 5, he received the Knight's Cross of the Iron Cross with Oak Leaves. (Private collection)

The Polish break out

The positions of the two companies (4 platoons) were quickly over-run. The reinforced Polish regiment launched an attempt to break out, and there was violent hand-to-hand combat in the sector of the line held by 11th Company. In just one hour, the Polish regimental train penetrated the open German lines and moved away to the south-east.

Oberstleutnant Sydow reported these developments to the air force commander for special operations in the presence of the commander

Horst Kerfin, in this photograph already an Oberleutnant, received the Knight's Cross of the Iron Cross on 24 May 1940 and was platoon leader in 11th Company. He was awarded the Iron Cross Second Class after the Sucha operation. (Private collection)

of 11th Company. The battalion commander also ordered the scattered remainders of 10th and 11th companies to be pulled together and placed on standby as battalion reserve.

The Polish train was later reported to have crossed the main road to Warsaw at Siekluki at around 01.30 hours. For the time being, the battle was over for Battalion III./Fallschirmjäger Regiment 1.

Oberstleutnant Sydow contacted 14th Army command in Radow and reported the events of the past day. He requested a reconnaissance unit to support reconnaissance, recovery and clean-up operations, but once again, the air force commander for special operations brought his influence to bear, and Sydow's request was denied.

Horst Kerfin fell on 22 January 1943 near Orel/Russia, with the rank of Hauptmann. Here, two paratroopers form the guard of honour for his coffin. (Janzyk)

Unlike most other soldiers of Battalion III, Kerfin came from the army's parachute infantry battalion. This photograph shows him with Alfred Schwarzmann. Both are wearing the paratrooper's qualification insignia of the army. (Janzyk)

After the battle

Clear-up and recovery operations in the Stawiszyn area began on 15 September at around 09.00 hours, following the arrival of lorries from Stuka squadron 77. The company secured the following:

- approximately 100 rifles
- six heavy machine guns with a plentiful supply of ammunition
- three mortars with ammunition
- thirty horses
- several vehicles
- two antitank rifles
- one orderly room chest
- one 3.7-cm cannon
- one ammunition carrier

Walter Heinkelein served in 9th Company under Oberleutnant Gessner. Shortly before the Invasion of Poland, he attended the parachute training school in Stendal, where he had to furnish a signed declaration of consent from his parents. (Janzyk)

Thus, Battalion III of Fallschirmjäger Regiment 1 was almost permanently engaged in battle with Polish forces from 09.30 on 14 September to 01.00 on 15 September 1939, leaving a total of thirteen dead and twenty-five wounded. According to the estimates and statements of inhabitants of the villages, approximately 150 Poles were killed and around 200 taken prisoner. Most of these Polish troops were from the 3rd Infantry Division, with some units from the 2nd Battalion of Infantry Regiment 8, who, on 10 September, had been ordered by their battalion commander, Major Koper, to break through and cross the Vistula.

Some of the fallen paratroopers were duly buried near the woods between Stawiszyn and Jasionna, others in the communal grave at the Sucha estate. The battalion surgeon tended to the wounded at the aid station on the Sucha estate until such time as they could be transported to the field hospitals at Radom.

Throughout this entire period, the battalion was without its train and had no vehicles of its own, lacked sufficient weapons, baggage and proper communications equipment, which made their situation even more difficult. They also had no field kitchens, which meant that between 12 September and the arrival of the battalion train in Sucha on 16 September, they hardly received any warm meals and were mainly dependent on the cold emergency rations they carried in their field bags.

After the battle at Sucha, Battalion III was only deployed once more, on a brief mission to the area 10 km north of Jetlinsk, where it was ordered by the air force commander for special operations to surround a piece of woodland. However, nothing worthy of mention occurred on this mission.

Since General von Richthofen had repeatedly overruled the decisions of the battalion commander, further deployment of the unit within this framework was out of the question. It was clear that General von Richthofen and Oberstleutnant Sydow had taken very different views on the deployment of the troops during the last few days. Otto Sydow never forgave air force commander for

Beſitz-Urkunde

em   **Oberjäger Ernſt Rattay**

    9./ Fallſchirm-Jäger Regiment 1

iſt auf Grund ſeiner am 14. 9. 1939 erlittenen

einmaligen Derwundung ~~oder Beſchädigung~~ das

Derwundeten-Abzeichen in ſchwarz

verliehen worden.

delegen, den 1. 12. 1939.

Oberſtleutnant und Batl. Kdr.

Oberjäger Ernst Rattay was wounded in the battle at Stawiszyn – Sucha on 14 September 1939, for which he was awarded the Verwundetenabzeichen (Wound Badge) in black by Oberstleutnant Sydow. (Private collection)

special operations General von Richthofen for bowing to pressure from superior command and sending his battalion into battle with undue haste and without reconnaissance. However, von Richthofen was expecting only scattered groups of Polish soldiers and not the battle-ready force of almost divisional strength which Sydow's men encountered.

Verleihungsurkunde

Ich verleihe dem

Oberjäger Ernst Rattay

das Abzeichen für

Fallschirmschützen

Berlin, den 24. November 193 9

Der Reichsminister der Luftfahrt
und Oberbefehlshaber der Luftwaffe

I.A.

Nr. 1736 /39   Generalmajor

The certificate of achievement awarded to Oberjäger Ernst Rattay with his paratrooper's qualification insignia. (Private collection)

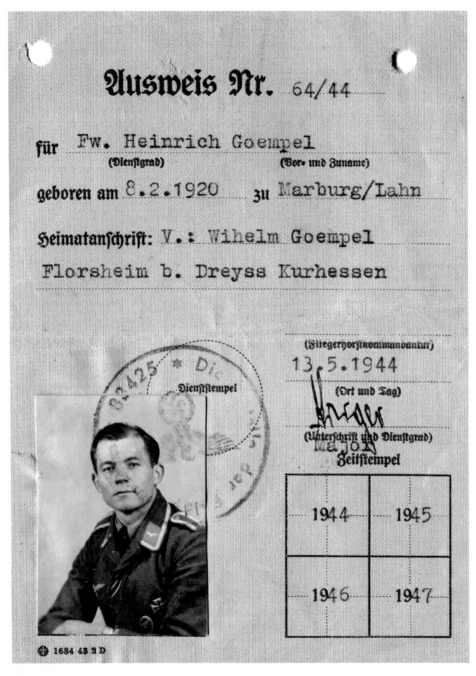

Heinrich Gömpel's Tarnausweis (special deceptive ID card carried on missions where capture by the enemy is likely) with his passport photograph. Paratroopers and airborne units usually received this ID card prior to a mission in exchange for their pay book, as the pay book would reveal much more information on the holder and his unit should it fall into enemy hands. (Private collection)

This application for the awarding of the Erdkampfabzeichen (Ground Assault badge) shows that Heinrich Gömpel took part in the battles in Poland as a member of 9th Company. The document was signed by Oberleutnant Merkordt and General Bräuer. (Private collection)

Return to Radom

The train of Battalion III arrived in Sucha on the evening of 6 September, and follow-up and the process of physical and mental recovery from their first mission began. Two days later, the battalion was transferred back to Radom at the request of the air force commander and was thus removed from von Richthofen's command.

II./FJR 1 was also engaged in battle with Polish forces, on 24 September 1939 at Wola Gulowska. At 10.00 hours, the regimental commander ordered Battalion III to advance to Wola Gulowska to provide back-up. However, when the battalion arrived at around 12.00, the battle was over, and the companies were only deployed to comb the woods together with Battalion II.

In early October, Battalion III returned to its peacetime barracks at Gardelegen, together with the rest of Fallschirmjäger Regiment 1. At a battalion inspection on 13 October 1939, General Student presented the Iron Cross Second Class medals and sent his paratroopers home on furlough.

Two paratroopers from 11th Company after their return to Gardelegen. (Janzyk)

Werner Zimmermann took part in the battle in the Sucha area when serving in 12th Company. This photograph shows Zimmermann as an Oberjäger after the Invasion of the Netherlands in 1940. He is wearing the embroidered paratrooper's qualification insignia on the breast of his service tunic. (Janzyk)

Werner Zimmermann's jump licence was issued before the Invasion of Poland. It is interesting that he continued to use it throughout the War, although there was no space left to enter later promotions. (Janzyk)

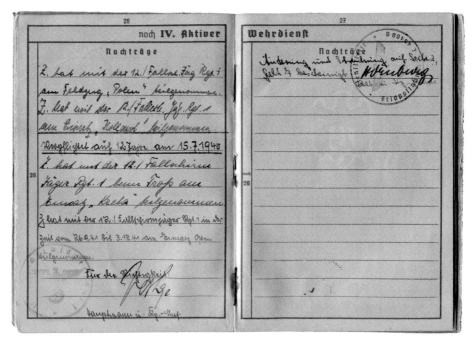

On page 26 of Werner Zimmermann's service record book, the later commander of 12th Company, Hauptmann Vosshage, confirms that Zimmermann took part in the Invasion of Poland. This would later be followed by entries for missions in 'Holland,' 'Crete' and on the 'Eastern Front.' The battles at Sucha and Wola Gulowska are listed on page 32. However, it should be mentioned that the men of Battalion III did not arrive in Wola Gulowska until after the battle. (Janzyk)

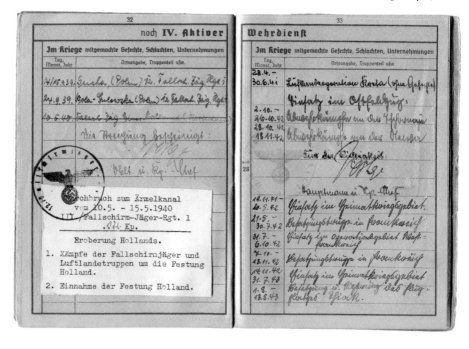

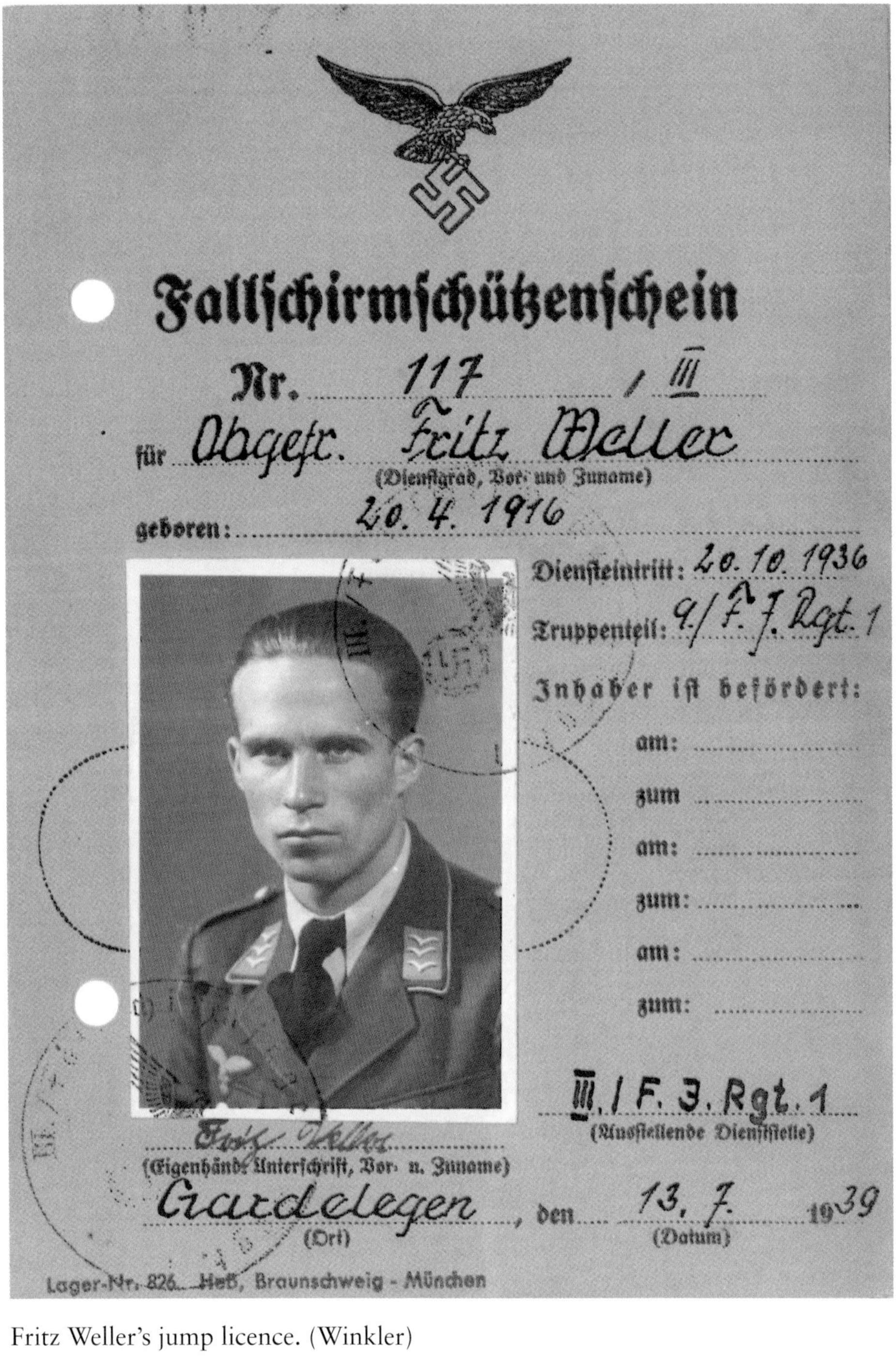

Fritz Weller's jump licence. (Winkler)

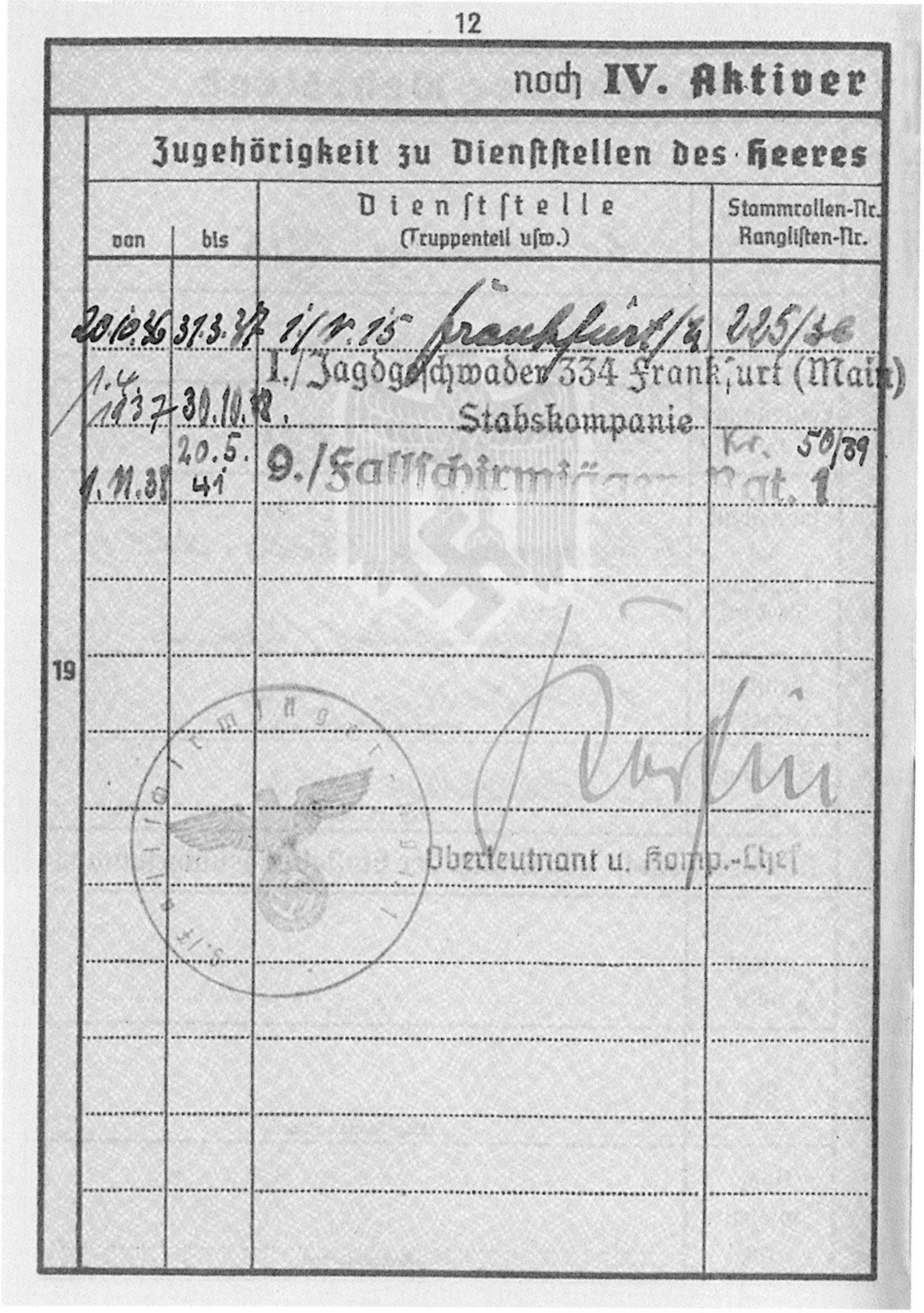

12

noch **IV. Aktiver**

Zugehörigkeit zu Dienststellen des Heeres

von	bis	Dienststelle (Truppenteil usw.)	Stammrollen-Nr. Ranglisten-Nr.
20.10.36	31.3.37	1/N.15 Frankfurt/M	225/36
1.4.37	30.10.38	I./Jagdgeschwader 334 Frankfurt (Main) Stabskompanie	
1.11.38	20.5. 41	9./Fallschirmjäger Bat. 1	Nr. 50/39

19

Oberleutnant u. Komp.-Chef

Page 12 of Fritz Weller's service record book shows which unit he was attached to at the time of the Invasion of Poland. (Winkler)

32

noch **IV. Aktiver**

Im Kriege mitgemachte Gefechte, Schlachten, Unternehmungen

Tag, Monat, Jahr	Ortsangabe, Truppenteil usw.
7.10.– 18.10.38.	*[handwritten]* J.J. Hr. Göring Sudetz.
17.3.– 21.3.39.	*[handwritten]*
12.9.– 6.10.39.	*[handwritten] Polen*
1.9.– 15.9.1.	*[handwritten]*
9.4.41.39.	*[handwritten]*
10.5.40 – 31.5.40	*[handwritten] Feldzug Holland*

[official seal] Oberleutnant u. Komp.-Chef

Fritz Weller saw action in the battle at Sucha as a paratrooper in 9th Company. When he fell on 21 May 1941 in Crete, his later company commander, Horst Kerfin, closed Weller's service record book with his signature and his official seal. (Winkler)

Chapter 4

I./Fallschirmjäger Regiment 1

Oberstleutnant Herbert Gratzy von Wardengg, a former officer of the Austrian air force, was commander of I./FJR 1 until the end of November 1939, when he was succeeded by Hauptmann Erich Walter. Gratzy became commander of the parachute training school in Wittstock. He died on 18 January 1940 during a failed attempt to open his parachute manually. In this photograph, he is wearing the 'Große Abendgesellschaftsanzug' (special evening dress uniform). A pilot's badge can be seen beneath the paratrooper qualification insignia. There are medals and decorations from the Austro-Hungarian Empire on his medal bar, headed by the Orden der Eisernen Krone (Order of the Iron Crown) and followed by the Militärverdienstkreuz (Military Merit Cross). (Janzyk)

On the move by air and vehicle convoy

Battalion I of Fallschirmjäger Regiment 1, under the command of Oberstleutnant Herbert Gratzy von Wardengg, was placed on the alert at the same time as its sister battalions and set out from Stendal in a vehicle convoy at 07.00 hours on 1 September 1939, with the destination of Seifersdorf near Legnica/Wroclaw.

In contrast to the two other battalions in the regiment, some paratroopers of the first battalion were airlifted to their operational air base. As there were some planes of Kampfgeschwader (bomber wing) for special operations 1 stationed in Stendal, some units of Battalion I were able to take advantage of the free transport space and fly to Legnica.

On arrival, they began with the now-familiar procedure of preparing the drop tanks. Each section type, for example staff, radio,

A photograph of the entire 4th/FJR 1, taken in the late summer of 1938. The company commander, sitting with his left leg crossed over his right, is Hauptmann Noster, who took command of Battalion I at the start of the formation of FJR 2. He was succeeded by Oberleutnant Gericke. The Zugführeroffiziere (platoon leading officers) next to him are Herbert Schmidt (left) and Alfred Genz (right). They were both awarded the Knight's Cross in the course of the War. It can also be clearly seen that almost all of the soldiers are wearing the stripes of the FJR 1 on their sleeves and the Luftwaffe paratrooper qualification insignia. (Janzyk)

engineers, infantry or light mortar section, used different inserts in these containers, which had to be packed with a precisely specified quantity of weaponry and equipment. A cargo parachute was attached to the upper side of the tank and coupled to the bomb release slips in the bomb racks of the Ju 52. Once the four tanks per plane had been lifted into the racks with the help of the mounting control stick and locked in place, a protective cap made from thin, perforated sheet metal to cushion the impact was attached to the underside of the tank, which was padded with a thick layer of felt.

The tanks were then released from the bomb racks when the paratroopers were dropped, floated down to the ground suspended from their cargo parachutes and, ideally, landed in the planned target area, enabling the troops to arm themselves immediately after landing.

For days, the transport planes stood on the runways, fully loaded and ready for take-off, but the order for a parachute mission was never issued. (Janzyk)

Paratroopers of 3rd/FJR 1 have been placed on the alert on the advanced airfield at Seifersdorf. Nevertheless, they have found the time to gather in front of one of the numerous Ju 52s for a souvenir photograph! (Janzyk)

The battalion's task was to report is readiness for action to the Regiment as quickly as possible. However, in Seifersdorf, too, the order to stand by was followed by days of waiting for further orders, and routine and boredom set in.

Deployment to the operational area

Following a divisional order on 19 September 1939, in the afternoon the paratroopers of I./FJR 1 began preparations for deployment to the Deblin area on the following morning.

On 20 September, beginning at 05.00 hours, the battalion, together with II./FJR 1, set out in endless columns of vehicles following a route which took it via Wroclaw – Radomsko – Radom – Zwolen – Pulawy to its assigned operational area near Deblin.

On the move into the operational area Deblin via vehicle convoy. During a brief stop shortly before Radom, the men of 1ˢᵗ/FJR 1 have the chance to stretch their legs. The paratrooper in the ditch is the later bearer of the Knight's Cross of the Iron Cross Erich Schuster. He is wearing the jump smock often nicknamed the 'Knochensack' (bone bag) over his uniform. (Janzyk)

Above: The convoy sets off again towards the east after just a few minutes. Altogether, the paratroopers travelled over 900 kilometres to their operational areas. (Janzyk)

Below: Arriving in Poland, the as yet inexperienced paratroopers are confronted with the destruction caused by war as the columns pass through one burnt-out village after another. (Janzyk)

An Oberleutnant on the battalion staff of Battalion I FJR 1 has been appointed coordinating officer. He is directing the convoy along the designated route at a junction of roads in a destroyed Polish village. The combination of one stripe and two wings on the top of the left sleeve of his 'bone bag' identify his rank. (Janzyk)

Above: Once again, waiting is the order of the day. Engineers need to prepare the bridge across the Vistula before the vehicle columns of I./ and II./FJR 1 can cross. The platoon of Rudolf Toschka (on the left next to the lorry), who will later be awarded the Knight's Cross of the Iron Cross, takes the opportunity to snap a few souvenir photos. Toschka is wearing a paratrooper's cartridge belt around his neck. This belt, together with a map case and a pair of field glasses, was issued to paratroopers instead of the standard leather ammunition pouch, which got in the way during a parachute drop. The Oberjäger on the far left on the bed of the lorry is Erwin Ellersiek. (Janzyk)

Below: A dynamited Polish wooden bridge on the road to Pulawy. The engineers have already constructed an emergency bridge, which can be seen in the background. (Janzyk)

Gathering the spoils of war

When they arrived in Deblin on 22 September 1939, the men were first quartered near the airfield to form a reserve contingent for 7th Fliegerdivision. The next morning, many of them seized the opportunity to take a look around the ruined airfield. On the afternoon of 23 September, the paratroopers of I./FJR 1 received orders to take charge of the recovery of tons of raw material and metals such as copper, zinc, lead, mercury, but also weapons and war material, which lay in storage on the Deblin airfield and in the casemates of the citadel of Ivangorod. It took the soldiers five days and nights to transport these vast amounts of material west, across the demarcation line, the Vistula river, on lorries. On 25 September, the reinforced I./FJR 2 arrived to support Oberstleutnant Gratzy's paratroopers. The purpose of this mission was to secure goods vital to the war effort for the German troops and prevent them being seized by Russian forces.

The Vistula river with the partly dynamited bridge near Pulawy. Once the army engineers had completed their task, the convoy moved off once more. (Janzyk)

Above: Paratroopers of 1/FJR 1 cross the Vistula in a convoy of lorries. (Janzyk)

Below: The bridge gate in Pulawy – the entry to the town via the bridge over the Vistula. (Janzyk)

Above: A wrecked Polish two-seater training plane manufactured by PWS, the Podlaska aircraft factory, photographed on the Deblin airfield on 23.9.39. (Janzyk)

Below: In addition to further raw materials, the Germans found tons of bars of copper, tin or brass on the Deblin airfield. (Private collection)

Above: A paratrooper examines the burnt-out metal shell of a Polish plane. (Private collection)

Below: The paratroopers of I./FJR 1 immediately began to secure the raw materials and goods, sorting them and preparing them for transport. However, the captured Polish planes which were still intact were of little military value, as they were outdated models. (Private collection)

Above: More seized Polish goods on Deblin airfield, including vast quantities of canons, guns, mortars and ammunition. (Janzyk)

Below: Soldiers of 1st/FJR 1, probably on kitchen detail, plucking geese during a break on the airfield at Deblin. Note that the first soldier is wearing an early M16 'bone bag,' the first model of the jump smock. The two Oberjäger are Helmut Arpke and Erwin Ellersiek. (Janzyk)

Above: Polish children watching a singing performance by the paratroopers near Deblin. They look rather sceptical, but unfortunately, it is not known whether this is due to the quality of the singing or because they do not understand German. (Janzyk)

Right: Hauptmann Koch, commander of 1st/FJR 1, with his men on Deblin airfield. (Janzyk)

Paratroopers peeling potatoes. Many of them had probably expected their first mission to be more exciting. However, this photograph shows a rare piece of equipment, the gas mask bag, which was introduced for paratroopers because the cylindrical metal canister which normally held the gas mask hindered them during an airdrop. (Janzyk)

Above: Oberjäger Ellersiek's group in Deblin, front of the mobile field kitchen, nicknamed the 'Gulaschkanone' (goulash cannon). The first soldier from the left, kneeling, is Ewald Hermet. The third from the right, standing, is Erich Schuster. A special feature of the paratroopers' weaponry can be seen in this photograph; as the soldiers jumped without the Karabiner 98k, each was armed with a Luger P08 for close range defence. (Janzyk)

Right: During the Invasion of Poland, Leutnant Gerhard Schacht was Zugführer of 1st platoon, 1st/FJR 1. After serving in the Polish campaign in 1939, he went on to fight on all fronts in the Second World War where paratroopers saw action, and was later awarded the Knight's Cross of the Iron Cross. In 1945, then a major, he was taken prisoner by the Allies in North Germany. (Janzyk)

Return to Germany

Much to the disappointment of the soldiers, Battalion I, Fallschirmjäger Regiment 1 saw no action or combat of any kind during the Invasion of Poland. On 28 September, they began their return journey to Germany via Pulawy and Radom, with a first stop at Kurzelow, where the troops of Battalion I were quartered from 29 September to 5 October. Starting on 5 October, they gathered with the rest of the 1ˢᵗ Regiment in Oppeln, and three days later, the paratroopers began the rail journey back to their home base in Stendal.

Erich Johannes Schuster was born in Morbach/Rhineland Palatinate in 1919. He joined the paratroopers in 1938 and signed up for jump training at the Stendal Parachute School in October of the same year. After the missions in Poland and on the Albert Canal, he took part in a parachute drop over Crete, during which the young Feldwebel proved himself so well that he was awarded the Knight's Cross of the Iron Cross.

Feldwebel SCHUSTER

Schuster was promoted to Leutnant on 1 July 1942. In this photograph, he is still wearing the uniform of a Feldwebel. He was placed in command of 1st Company FJR 5 and immediately deployed to Africa with his troops. Erich Schuster fell on 11 January 1941 at Medjez el Bab (Tunisia), at the foot of Hill 311. (Janzyk)

Above: After his speech, Hauptmann Koch discusses further procedures with his two platoon leading officers, Leutnant Gerhard Schacht and Leutnant Martin Schächter. In May 1940, all three officers were awarded the Knight's Cross of the Iron Cross for distinguished service in Belgium. (Janzyk)

Below: During their return journey, I./FJR 1 took up quarters in Kurzelow from 29 September to 5 October. This photograph shows the company commander of 1ˢᵗ/FJR 1, Hauptmann Walter Koch, and his soldiers. The commander is addressing the inhabitants of Kurzelow. (Janzyk)

Above: One of the buildings in which 1st/FJR 1 was quartered in Kurzelow. A sentry stands guard in front of the building. (Janzyk)

Below: The paratroopers quickly set to work to decorate the walls of their quarters. Note also how fastidiously the equipment has been set down and the steel paratrooper helmets, which were introduced in 1938. (Janzyk)

'Dreaming by a Polish fireside', drawn by Walter Baedge, a soldier in 1ˢᵗ/FJR 1 who later became group leader of the Sturmabteilung (storm trooper detachment) Koch. (Janzyk)

With only their regular duties to keep them occupied, boredom slowly began to set in, and the men hoped that they would soon return to Stendal. (Janzyk)

I./FJR 1 passed through Opole on 5 October 1939 and was given a warm welcome by the inhabitants. This administrative district in Silesia profited directly from the annexation of Polish territory and was restructured and enlarged in the course of the same year. (Janzyk)

A last souvenir photo of Rudolf Toschka's platoon before it boarded the train to return to Stendal. The photograph shows several later bearers of the Knight's Cross of the Iron Cross, among them Toschka himself, Helmut Arpke, Erich Schuster and Wilhelm Kempke. Also present are Ewald Hermet, Fritz Pohlmann (with dog), Erwin Ellersiek, Erich Rückriem and Rudolf Barding. (Janzyk)

Reading the newspaper in Opole. Some of the paratroopers were even able to visit acquaintances or relatives in the Silesian town. This Gefreiter is wearing a loop made of braid around his epaulette, which shows that he is an Unteroffiziersan-wärter (candidate for noncommissioned rank). (Janzyk)

Erich Rückriem joined Regiment General Göring in Berlin on 4 November 1937. The 'Waffenfarbe' (corps colour) of this unit was white. Note the blue sleeve stripe with the embroidered lettering in matt grey. (Private collection)

Following the reclassification of parts of the RGG as I./FJR 1 and the move to Stendal, Rückriem was promoted to Gefreiter on 1 December 1938. This photograph shows him wearing the paratrooper qualification insignia, awarded in August 1938. After the Invasion of Poland, Erich Rückriem became an Oberjäger. Rückriem commanded Trupp 9 of Sturmgruppe Stahl in Sturmabteilung Koch and received the Iron Cross First Class for distinguished service at the Albert Canal. (Private collection)

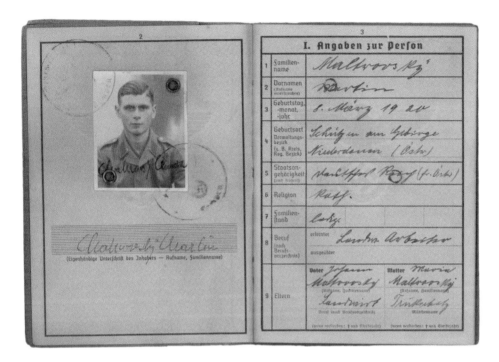

Above: Martin Maltrovsky began his military career in 1938 with 9th Regiment SA-Standarte Feldherrenhalle and joined 3rd Company, Fallschirmjäger Regiment 1 in 1939, in which he served until being taken prisoner in 1945. He reached the rank of Leutnant and fought in Poland, Norway, Holland, Crete, Russia and Italy without ever being wounded. Maltrovsky was awarded both the Deutsches Kreuz (German Cross) in Gold and the Nahkampfspange (Close Combat Clasp) in Bronze. (Skvaril)

Overleaf above: Prior to the mission in Poland, in the summer of 1939, Gefreiter Maltrovsky attended the Stendal Parachute School. However, he did not receive his paratrooper's qualification insignia until January 1940. Page 20 of his service record book certifies that he received training in the use of the typical infantry weapons ranging from the Karabiner 98 kurz, the Luger P08, light machine guns, submachine guns right through to hand grenades. (Skvaril)

Overleaf below: Martin Maltrovsky's service record book confirms his participation in the Invasion of Poland with 3rd Company of FJR 1. FJR1 was not engaged in combat of any kind, which is also correspondingly documented. (Skvaril)

20 — noch IV. Aktiver

Ausbildung (auch im Kriege)

Mit der Waffe: Karab. 98 u. Pistole 08 z. 1. 9. 34

u. f. Handgranate

21 — Wehrdienst

Ausbildung (auch im Kriege)

Sonstige Ausbildung, Lehrgänge:

Fallschirmschützenlehrgang Wittstock
31.6. – 30.7.39

U.- Lehrgang v. 8. – 24.3.1941

Zugführerlehrgang bei Waffenschule der
Oberkfehlshaben Südwest vom 28.10. – 2.12.44

1.4. – 1.5.45 K.O.N.-Lehrgang
(Fahnenschule I. Fsch. Korps)

Abzeichen usw. (auch im Kriege):
Fallschirmschützenabzeichen f. F. Schützen verl. am 20.6.40

32 — noch IV. Aktiver

Im Kriege mitgemachte Gefechte, Schlachten, Unternehmungen

Tag Monat Jahr	Ortsangabe, Truppenteil usw.
20.9. 5.10.39	Teilnahme am Einsatz Polen. Kein Gefecht 3./Fallschirm-Jäger Regt. 1
9.4. – 11.4.40	Teilnahme am Einsatz Stavanger / Sola Maschine infolge Unwetterheit notgelandet
10.5. – 20.5.40	Teilnahme am Einsatz Dordrecht / Holland Gefecht um Dordrecht
15.5. – 21.6.40	Teilnahme am Einsatz Narvik. Gefechte
	3./Fallschirm-Jäger Regt. 1

33 — 32a — Im Kriege mitgem. Gefechte

25.11 – 16.12.42	Winterschlacht um den Bereich der 9. Armee
17.12. – 15.2.43	Abwehrkämpfe im Bereich der 9. Armee
1.2. – 31.3.43	Schlacht im Orelbogen
9.7. – 11.9.43	Sicherung Mittel- u. Süditalien
12.9. – 20.11.43	Abwehrkämpfe i. Süditalien u. Absetzen auf Sangro-Stellung
21.11.43 – 11.5.44	Abwehrkämpfe i. Mittelitalien
28.11. – 27.12.43	Abwehrschlacht a. Sangro
28.12.43 – 7.2.44	Abwehrschlacht u. Ortona
8.2. – 18.2.44	1. Abwehrschlacht b. Cassino
15.3. – 24.3.44	2. Abwehrschlacht b. Cassino
12.5. –	Abwehrschlachten in Mittelitalien
25.8.44	u. Rückzugskämpfe auf den nördl. Apennin

Chapter 5

I./Fallschirmjäger Regiment 2

This group photograph shows the officer corps of Oberleutnant Morawetz' 4th Company in August 1939. It is not known why all paratroopers have removed their paratrooper's qualification insignia, but a number of familiar faces can be identified. Front row from left to right: unidentified, unidentified, Feldwebel Windisch (parachute infantry battalion), Oberleutnant Wolf, Oberleutnant Morawetz, Oberleutnant Lüdke, Leutnant Hasseldiek (parachute infantry company), unidentified, unidentified, unidentified. (Janzyk)

Deblin-Irena airfield was almost totally destroyed by German bombers. The majority of Polish planes and vehicles left were no more than burnt-out wrecks. (Janzyk)

Forming the reserve in Gardelegen

Sadly, sources of information on the early deployment of Fallschirmjäger Regiment 2 (which was intended to be the equivalent of 1st Regiment as regards its basic composition) during the Invasion of Poland are far rarer than in the case of Fallschirmjäger Regiment 1. Nevertheless, this young regiment, the formation of which did not begin until early 1939, and its two battalions were involved in the Polish campaign.

When the order to stand by was received from 7th Fliegerdivision, Battalion I initially remained in its home base Gardelegen as a reserve. As parts of II./FJR 2 had been placed under Luftwaffe Supreme Command, the battalion was brought up to strength by the addition of 5th and 6th companies.

Late deployment

For the paratroopers, the Polish campaign began on 12 September 1939 with their relatively late relocation to the operational air bases around Legnica. By this time, III./FJR 1 was on its way to Radom, while I./FJR 2 was to move forward and take its place in the event of a parachute mission.

Securing the spoils of war

On 20 September 1939, I./ and II./FJR 1 left their operational air bases in the Legnica/Wroclaw area. Five days later, I./FJR 2 followed and was airlifted to the Irena-Deblin airfield. Here, Hauptmann Noster's paratroopers were ordered to support I./FJR 1, which had already arrived there, in securing raw materials and goods in the Deblin area. Working day and night, on lorries from I./FJR 1, they transported mercury, copper, tin and other precious metals westwards from the citadel of Ivangorod, which was located east of the Vistula, and from Deblin airfield across the bridges over the Vistula near Pulawy.

Redeployment

I./FJR left the operational area at the end of September, together with parts of the 1st Regiment. It was not involved in combat during its mission in Poland and therefore suffered no losses. Back in Gardelegen, the formation and training of the young battalion continued.

Oberjäger Walter Eberz from I./FJR 2 in front of the Lublin Gate of the fortress of Ivangorod. (Janzyk)

Above: An unidentified paratrooper of I./FJR 2 on Deblin-Irena airfield, lost in thought as he surveys the destruction and ruin wrought by explosions. (Janzyk)

Below: The operational area of I./FJR 2 at the citadel of Ivangorod, where tons of raw materials were stored. The task of the paratroopers was to secure these materials. The man in the foreground of this photograph is wearing a yellow armband with 'Deutsche Wehrmacht' in black letters, identifying him as a member of the Reichsarbeitsdienst (RAD) (Reich Labour Service), which was under the control of the military. (Private collection)

Chapter 6

II./Fallschirmjäger Regiment 2

Deployment to Slovakia

There is also very little information available about the involvement of
II./Fallschirmjäger Regiment 2 under Hauptmann Erich Pietzonka. It
is known that the battalion, which was not formed until June 1939,
in Tangermünde, was not yet prepared for an airdrop, that is, that the
majority of the companies had not yet absolved their parachute training at
this time. There were also considerable deficits in their infantry training.
For this reason, the commander of the 7th Fliegerdivision, General Kurt
Student, decided to assign the battalion to Luftwaffe Supreme Command
and not to consider it for any possible mission of his division.

Luftwaffe Supreme Command airlifted Battalion II to Zipser-
Neudorf in eastern Slovakia on 28 August 1939. The battalion's
mission was to secure a German air base for fighter planes and long-
range fighters for the imminent invasion of Poland and to prevent any
Polish units breaking through over the Tatra Mountains. As 5th and
6th companies had already been assigned to Hauptmann Noster's
Battalion I, however, only the battalion staff, 7th and 8th companies
participated in this mission.

Wehrmacht command justified the deployment of this fully armed
and equipped combat force by claiming that a mutiny was planned
within the Slovakian military. They stated that a coup d'état was
about to be launched and that the paratroopers were therefore being
sent to protect the Slovakian leader, who sympathised with Hitler
Germany. This was, of course, a fabrication.

Back-up tasks in Poland

On 9 and 10 October, units of II./Fallschirmjäger Regiment 2 were
transferred to Krosno in southern Poland in a vehicle convoy. There,
the under-strength battalion received orders from Luftwaffe Supreme

Command to assume further back-up missions on the Dukla Pass and in Sanok in Southern Poland. These missions, however, produced no significant results.

8th/FJR 2 was also ordered to secure planes located at the nearby Polish glider airfield in Przemyśl and to load them up for transport to Germany.

Battalion II returned to its peacetime barracks in Tangermünde in October without having seen action.

Summary

Baptism of fire

Battalions II and III of Fallschirmjäger Regiment 1 received their baptism of fire in Poland in September 1939. Other units such as the two 1st battalions of the regiments were merely assigned the mission of securing raw materials and important war material in transport operations lasting several days.

Despite an airdrop being scheduled three times, the original plan for the paratrooper units to carry out a swift initial operation by dropping infantry troops behind the enemy lines was never put into action. As described above, on two of these occasions the paratroopers were already sitting in their planes on the operational air bases, armed and ready for action, only to receive the order to stand down.

The fact that no airdrops were carried out led to perceptible demotivation and gloom among the troops, prompting many of them to apply for transfers on their return to their peacetime barracks. The end of 1939/beginning of 1940 saw many of them, and this is true across all ranks, back in the infantry or engineer units from which they had originally volunteered for transfer to the paratroopers.

Disappointment

Disappointment is said to have been particularly strong in I./Fallschirmjäger Regiment 1, as the vast majority of the men serving here were first-generation paratroopers who had received their parachute training in 1936 or 1937. Their motivation was correspondingly high, yet in contrast to the other two battalions of the regiment, who at least saw action, they were given no opportunity to prove their worth. In their eyes, the military skills they had acquired in years of training were wasted and their potential squandered.

Confidence in the higher leadership levels was particularly badly shaken in Battalion III of Fallschirmjäger Regiment 1. The men not only witnessed the conflict between General von Richthofen and Oberstleutnant Sydow, but experienced its effects at first hand when the air force commander for special operations sent them into action against an enemy force of unknown strength without warning and without prior reconnaissance, in contradiction of all procedural directives.

The relatively high losses they suffered as a result were attributed not to the military skill of the enemy but to the ignorance and stubbornness of General von Richthofen, who repeatedly and blatantly ignored the requests and suggestions of the battalion's own commander as to how the mission should be conducted.

Apparently as a result of the obvious failure of the mission, there are no photographic records of the battle or of the graves of the fallen from Battalion III, providing a stark contrast to the case of the battle at Wola Gulowska, of which there are a great number of photographs showing not only the battle itself but also the burials and the cemetery in the Fortress of Ivangorod.

However, as the men of Battalion III were sent into action in great haste and only lightly equipped against enemy forces which, just one day later, were found to be unexpectedly superior, they probably had more pressing concerns than taking snapshots. In contrast, the mission at Wola Gulowska was well prepared in advance and executed with less haste.

The cover story

The widespread claim that the order for a parachute mission was not issued due to a desire to keep the existence of this new type of military unit secret is simply wrong. After all, the paratroopers were already sitting in their planes and ready to go into action twice. The rapid advance of the army and positive developments on the front lines were major factors which prevented the deployment of the paratroopers.

Moreover, both the Russian army command and British military intelligence were already aware of the existence of a German airborne force.

Conclusion

It can nevertheless be said that despite all hindrances, the first mission of the paratroopers went to the full satisfaction of their superior officers. Although the organisation phase was in some cases not yet complete, all battalions completed their missions. Their long and intensive training before the War made them particularly effective in unexpected and unanticipated combat situations.

Just six months later, the soldiers of 7th Fliegerdivision would once again be sitting on board their Ju 52s or transport gliders, ready to open the Westfeldzug (Battle of France) – code name 'FALL GELB' (CASE YELLOW).

Appendices

Staffing of 7th Fliegerdivision – September 1939

7th Fliegerdivision	Based in Berlin Tempelhof
Commander:	Generalmajor Student
Aide-de-camp:	Hauptmann Pilger
Ia:	Major i. General-Stab Erhard
Ia op.1:	Major Heidrich
	Hauptmann Trettner
	Hauptmann Küster
	Leutnant von Roon
Ia op.2:	Major Reinberger
	Hauptmann Vogel
Ic:	Hauptmann Scheuplein
	Oberleutnant Lampertsdörfer
Ic and Ib 2:	Major Dallmann
	Hauptmann Kähtler
Ib 1:	Major Winde
Liason Officers:	Hauptmann Schostag
	Leutnant Senger
II and IIa:	Oberstleutnant von Fichte
IIb:	Major (E) Ehrlich
Divisional surgeon:	Oberstabsarzt Dr. Knaebel
Headquarters squadron:	Oberleutnant Schäfer
Reconnaissance squadron:	Oberleutnant Langguth
FallschPakKp (antitank gun company):	Hauptmann Götzel
Transport company:	Hauptmann Rohloff
Artillery supply unit:	Oberleutnant Schram
Transport glider supply unit:	Leutnant Kiess

Signal company:	Oberleutnant Schleicher
Medical platoon:	Stabsarzt Dr. Neumann
Task force for sp. ops. 1:	Oberstleutnant Morzik
Task force for sp. ops. 2:	Oberstleutnant Drewes

Fallschirmjäger Regiment 1

Commander	Oberst Bräuer
Adjutant:	Hauptmann Graf von der Schulenburg

Battalion I	**Based in Stendal**
Commander:	Oberstleutnant Gratzy von Wardegg
1st Company:	Hauptmann Koch
2nd Company:	Hauptmann Gröschke
3rd Company:	Oberleutnant Götte
4th Company:	Hauptmann Gericke

Battalion II	**Based in Braunschweig**
Commander:	Hauptmann Prager
Engineer platoon:	Oberleutnant Witzig
5th Company:	Oberleutnant Herrmann
6th Company:	Oberleutnant Stangenberg
7th Company:	Oberleutnant Pagels
8th Company:	Oberleutnant Pelz

Battalion III	**Based in Gardelegen**
Commander:	Oberstleutnant Sydow
9th Company:	Oberleutnant Gessner
10th Company:	Oberleutnant Dunz
11th Company:	Oberleutnant Becker
12th Company:	Hauptmann Schmidt

Fallschirmjäger Regiment 2

Commander:	Oberst Sturm

Battalion I   **Based in Gardelegen**
Commander: Hauptmann Noster
1st Company: Oberleutnant Schlichting
2nd Company: Hauptmann Merten
3rd Company: Oberleutnant von Roon
4th Company: Hauptmann Morawetz

Battalion II   **Based in Tangermünde**
Commander: Hauptmann Pietzonka
5th Company: Oberleutnant Thiel
6th Company: Oberleutnant Schirmer
7th Company: Oberleutnant Schwarz
8th Company: Oberleutnant Paul

Files on troop losses were kept by the Wehrmachtsauskunftstelle für Kriegerverluste und Kriegsgefangene (WASt) (Wehrmacht agency maintaining records of personnel killed in action and prisoners of war), founded on 26 August 1939 in Berlin. Under § 77 of the Geneva Convention, all countries at war were required to set up such an agency. Its primary function was to register and report all enemy personnel interned as prisoners of war. The WASt, which was under Wehrmacht high command in the Deutsche Reich, was also responsible for maintaining records of German personnel killed in action. For this reason, the 'Deutsche Dienststelle' – as the WASt has been known since January 1946 – still has extensive files on military personnel. These are constantly updated and can be accessed for research purposes or to obtain information on missing family members.

II./Fallschirmjäger Regiment 1 - Losses
Fallen:
Bader, Hans

Rank:	Gefreiter	
Unit:	8th/FJR 1	Böhmler detachment
Date/place of birth:	1 April 1917	Ehingen
Date/place of death:	24 Sept. 1939	village of Wola Gulowska

Blum, Heinrich

Rank:	Gefreiter	
Unit:	8th/FJR 1	Böhmler detachment
Date/place of birth:	9 Oct. 1919	Cologne
Date/place of death:	24 Sept. 1939	village of Wola Gulowska

Holländer, Ferdinand

Rank:	Gefreiter	
Unit:	6th/FJR 1	Böhmler detachment
Date/place of birth:	11 June 1920	Linz
Date/place of death:	24 Sept. 1939	village of Wola Gulowska

Lorenz, Hans

Rank:	Obergefreiter	
Unit:	8th/FJR 1	Böhmler detachment
Date/place of birth:	15 Nov. 1919	Burgwall
Date/place of death:	24 Sept. 1939	village of Wola Gulowska

Martens, Hans

Rank:	Gefreiter	
Unit:	Engineer platoon II./Fallschirmjäger Regiment 1	
Date/place of birth:	28 March 1916	Kiel
Date/place of death:	24 Sept. 1939	north of Wola Gulowska during attack on the forest

Mensch, Kurt

Rank:	Feldwebel	
Unit:	5th/FJR 1	
Date/place of birth:	30 Nov. 1911	Oberstein
Date/place of death:	24 Sept. 1939	near Wola Gulowska following an accident with his submachine gun

Morcinek, Hans

Rank:	Oberjäger	
Unit:	Staff II./FJR 1	
Date/place of birth:	6 May 1913	Gleiwitz
Date/place of death:	24 Sept. 1939	north of Wola Gulowska during attack on the forest

Wiese, Albert

Rank:	Gefreiter	
Unit:	8th/FJR 1	Böhmler detachment
Date/place of birth:	9 Sept. 1919	Duisburg
Date/place of death:	24 Sept. 1939	village of Wola Gulowska

Later died of their injuries:
Cyron, Paul

Unit:	Staff II./FJR 1
Died:	11 Dec. 1939

Kobisch, Lothar

Unit:	8th/FJR 1
Died:	6 Nov. 1939

Discharged due to injury:
Fröhlig, Erich

Unit:	6th/FJR 1
Date of discharge:	11 Nov. 1939

Hirschfeld, Ewald

Unit:	7th/FJR 1
Date of discharge:	9 Nov. 1939

Höbelmann, Albert

Unit:	7th/FJR 1
Date of discharge:	9 Nov. 1939

These colour photographs of the funeral ceremony in the Fortress of Ivangorod were taken by Gerhard Becker, a member of the Witzig engineer platoon. (Private collection)

Kruczeck, August
Unit: 5th/FJR 1
Date of discharge: 10 Nov. 1939

Kunath, Herbert
Unit: 8th/FJR 1
Date of discharge: 21 Nov. 1939

Meyer, Karl
Unit: 6th/FJR 1
Date of discharge: 11 Nov. 1939

Pätz, Wilhelm
Unit: 6th/FJR 1
Date of discharge: 11 Nov. 1939

Stubbs, Werner
Unit: 7th/FJR 1
Date of discharge: 25 Jan. 1940

Zapatka, Eduard
Unit: 8th/FJR 1
Date of discharge: 6 Nov. 1939

III./Fallschirmjäger Regiment 1 - Losses

Fallen:
Thöle, Herbert
Rank: Gefreiter
Unit: 9th/FJR 1
Date/place of birth: 28 Feb. 1918   Delmenhorst
Date/place of death: 14 Sept. 1939   Stawiszyn

Kornet, Alfred Heinrich
Rank: Obergefreiter
Unit: 9ᵗʰ/FJR 1
Date/place of birth: 22 Feb. 1916   Schonnebeck
Date/place of death: 14 Sept. 1939   Stawiszyn

Winner, Karl
Rank: Jäger
Unit: 9ᵗʰ/FJR 1
Date/place of birth: 1 Feb. 1918   Oestnich
Date/place of death: 14 Sept. 1939   Stawiszyn

Lenzen, Arnold
Rank: Jäger
Unit: 9ᵗʰ/FJR 1
Date/place of birth: 25 Feb. 1918   Langerwehr
Date/place of death: 14 Sept. 1939   Stawiszyn

Henze, Helmut
Rank: Jäger
Unit: 9ᵗʰ/FJR 1
Date/place of birth: 24 June 1918   Iserlohn
Date/place of death: 14 Sept. 1939   Stawiszyn

Nitsch, Bruno
Rank: Oberjäger
Unit: 10ᵗʰ/FJR 1
Date/place of birth: 27 April 1914   Burgersdorf
Date/place of death: 14 Sept. 1939   Stawiszyn

Hess, Heribert
Rank: Oberjäger
Unit: 10ᵗʰ/FJR 1
Date/place of birth: 26 June 1919   Legau
Date/place of death: 14 Sept. 1939   Stawiszyn

Förster, Heinz

Rank:	Obergefreiter	
Unit:	10th/FJR 1	
Date/place of birth:	13 July 1912	Viersen/Rhineland
Date/place of death:	14 Sept. 1939	Stawiszyn

Kemper, Otto

Rank:	Obergefreiter	
Unit:	10th/FJR 1	
Date/place of birth:	2 Oct. 1915	Poznan
Date/place of death:	14 Sept. 1939	Stawiszyn

Steiner, Ludwig

Rank:	Gefreiter	
Unit:	10th/FJR 1	
Date/place of birth:	13 June 1915	Nuremberg
Date/place of death:	14 Sept. 1939	Stawiszyn

Seide, Hermann Richard

Rank:	Jäger	
Unit:	10th/FJR 1	
Date/place of birth:	26 Oct. 1919	Neuteich
Date/place of death:	14 Sept. 1939	Stawiszyn

Winckelmann, Nikolaus

Rank:	Jäger	
Unit:	10th/FJR 1	
Date/place of birth:	5 Sept. 1918	Flensburg
Date/place of death:	14 Sept. 1939	Stawiszyn

Dollase, Benno

Rank:	Jäger	
Unit:	10th/FJR 1	
Date/place of birth:	22 April 1921	Wiesental
Date/place of death:	14 Sept. 1939	Stawiszyn

Gedenke im Gebete
des ehrengeachteten
Herrn

Josef Neulinger

von Höhenberg
Obergefreiter in einem
Fallschirmjäger-Regiment
welcher am 6. Okt. 1939
im Feldlazarett Radom
in Polen an Ruhrerkran-
kung, in einem Alter von
27 Jahren fürs Vaterland
starb.

Ehre seinem Andenken!

Wer für Freiheit gab sein Blut,
Ruht auch in fremder Erde gut

Druck: Hans Treichler. Tittling

Du hast gekämpft fürs Vaterland,
Wie war der Abschied schwer.
Nun ruhest Du im Feindesland,
Wir seh'n uns hier nicht mehr.
Heißgeliebter, ruh' im Frieden,
Die fremde Erde sei Dir leicht.
Wir tragen gern, was Gott beschieden
Auch unser Weg nach oben zeigt

The lists shown here only include those who were killed in action or later died as a result of their wounds. Obergefreiter Josef Neulinger died in Kriegslazarett 2/571 Radom on 6 October 1939, of dysentery, which he probably contracted during the Invasion of Poland. He served in 10th Company, Bataillon I. (Private collection)

Later died of their injuries:
Bigge, Heinz

Rank:	Obergefreiter
Unit:	10th/FJR 1
Date of death:	17 Sept. 1939

No members of staff, 11th or 12th Company were killed or seriously wounded.

Polish troops of II./1st PAC killed in action (verified):

Kanonier	**Brylka**
Plutonowy	**Jan Dmitryszyn**
Kapitan	**Jan Zdzislaw Hennig** - commander of 5th battery
Kanonier	**Jan Matuszkiewicz**

Plutonowy	**Michal Michalczuk**
Podporucznik. Rez	**Józef Walenty Piaskunowicz**
Bombardier	**Leon Raflaski**
Kanonier	**Antoni Rastenis**
Kapitan	**Józef Sobczak** – commander of 6th battery
Kanonier	**Józef Sobiecki**
Kanonier	**Marian Trzaska**

Personnel awarded the Iron Cross Second Class for outstanding service in the Invasion of Poland in 1939

7th Fliegerdivison	**Kurt Student**	
FJR 1	**Bruno Bräuer**	
I./FJR 1	**Kurt Gröschke**	(2nd/FJR 1)
II./FJR 1	**Fritz Prager**	
	Willy Rohrbach	(5th/FJR 1)
	Rudolf Böhmler	(8th/FJR 1)
	Hans Fugmann	(5th/FJR 1)
	Andreas Hagl	(8th/FJR 1)
	Heinz Weithase	(7th/FJR 1)
III./FJR 1	**Otto Sydow**	
	Karl Heinz Becker	(11th/FJR 1)
	Horst Trebes	(9th/FJR 1)
	Horst Kerfin	(11th/FJR 1)
	Werner Dunz	(10th/FJR 1)
	Helmut Wagler	(Staff)
	Werner Isenberg	(11th/FJR 1)

Due to the lack of a verified sources, this list is unfortunately very incomplete. It has been compiled on the basis of literary, photographic and documentary research. Presumably, the fallen paratroopers were awarded the Iron Cross Second Class posthumously, but it has only been possible to verify this in two cases (Bader and Morcinek).

Above: Following their return to Braunschweig, thirteen paratroopers of II./FJR 1 receive the Iron Cross Second Class for distinguished service from General Student and Bruno Bräuer. (Private collection)

Below: This photograph shows the men of III./FJR 1 receiving the Iron Cross Second Class.
Left to right: Becker, Wagler, Trebes, Isenberg, rest unknown.

Colour photographs taken by Gerhard Becker

During the Invasion of Poland, Gerhard Becker served in the Witzig engineer platoon. During the lorry convoy and after the battle of Wola Gulowska, he took unique photographs of the village and the bridge over the Vistula at Pulawy, as well as of the funeral ceremony for his fallen comrades in the Fortress of Ivangorod. These photographs are placed at the end of this book without comment, so that they speak with their colours alone.

Colour photography had been possible since the 1860s, but as it was a technologically complex process, only few photographers were skilled enough to use it, and it could only be used for static motifs. In 1902, the German technicians Adolf Miethe and Adolf Traube developed a process for panchromatic sensitisation of the film material, but it was not until 1935 that Kodak put a tripack film suitable for mass use on the market. Further development in Germany led to the introduction in 1936 of the Agfacolor film, which was produced in the Agfa works in Wolfen in the province of Saxony and was to revolutionise the future of photography.

Sources

Federal Archive

RL 33 – 249   War diary of II./Fallschirmjäger Regiment 1 from
               19 August – 13 October
               1939

RL 33 – 249   Report on the reconnaissance mission of 1st pla-
               toon of 6th Company on 23 September 1939

RL 33 – 249   Combat report of II./Fallschirmjäger Regiment 1
               on the battle of Wola Gulowska on 24 September
               1939

BW 37 – 83   Report on battle of III./Fallschirmjäger Regiment 1
               on 14 and 15 September 1939 in the area of Suski
               Mlynek–Jasionna–Witassyn–Branica–Stawiszyn

N 671 – 4   War diary of air force commander for
               special operations General von Richthofen,
               12 September – 5 October 1939

Private collection
Company diary, 11th/Fallschirmjäger Regiment 1, 1939

Bibiliography

Busch, Erich, *Die Fallschirmjäger – Chronik 1935 – 1945* (Podzun-Pallas Verlag, Friedberg 1983)

Franz, Thomas and Wegmann Günther, *Die Ritterkreuzträger der deutschen Wehrmacht 1939-1945, Teil 2 Fallschirmjäger* (Biblio Verlag, Bissendorf 1986)

Golla, Karl Heinz, *Die deutsche Fallschirmtruppe 1936-1941* (Verlag E.S. Mittler & Sohn, Hamburg 2006)

Götzel, Hermann, *Generaloberst Kurt Student und seine Fallschirm-jäger* (Podzun-Pallas Verlag, Friedberg 1980)

Hönscheid, Johannes M., *Himmel und Hölle. Das Kriegstagebuch des Fallschirmjägers Martin Pöppel* (Internationaler Kulturdienst Verlag GmbH, Munich 1985)

Kameradschaft FJR 2, *Die Geschichte des Fallschirmjäger Regiment 2* (Self-publication)

Kühn, Volkmar, *Deutsche Fallschirmjäger im 2. Weltkrieg* (Motor-buch Verlag, Stuttgart 1985)

Nasse, Jean Yves, *Grüne Teufel! Die deutsche Fallschirmtruppe 1939-1945* (VDM Nickel, Zweibrücken 1997)

Nasse, Jean Yves, *Fallschirmjäger auf Kreta* (Motorbuch Verlag, Stuttgart 2006)

Peter, Klaus J., *Fallschirmjäger Regiment 3. Band 1: Vom Sturm-bataillon zum Regiment 1916-1941*, (Bender Publishing, San Jose 1992)

Queen, Eric, *Red Shines the Sun* (Bender Publishing, San Jose 2002)

Roth, Günter, *Die deutsche Fallschirmtruppe 1936-1945* (Verlag E.S. Mittler & Sohn, Hamburg 2010)

Traditionskameradschaft 11ᵗʰ/Fallschirmjäger Regiment 1, *Broschüre zum Treffen 1978 in Neustadt am Aisch* (Self-publication 1978)

Villahermosa, Gilberto, *Hitler's Paratrooper – The Life and Battles of Rudolf Witzig* (Frontline Books, London 2010)

Von Roon, Arnold, *Die Bildchronik der Fallschirmtruppe* (Nebel Verlag, Utting 2008)

About the Author

Stephan Janzyk, born in 1985, comes from Hagenow in Mecklenburg/Western Pomerania. He is an officer in the parachute regiment and holds a Master of Arts in educational sciences. He wrote his thesis on the subject of the socialisation aspects of the Hitler Youth in relation to a later career as an officer in the Wehrmacht. Stephan Janzyk has been interested in military history for many years, in particular in the formation and the early years of the German paratrooper units.